FANTASTIC 4

THE MAKING OF THE MOVIE

FANTASTIC FOUR: THE MAKING OF THE MOVIE
1 84576 083 2

Published by
Titan Books
A division of
Titan Publishing Group Ltd
144 Southwark St
London
SE1 0UP

First edition July 2005
2 4 6 8 10 9 7 5 3 1

Acknowledgements
The publishers would like to thank everyone who helped make this book possible, in particular our liaisons with Marvel and Twentieth Century Fox: Iain Wakefield, David Gorder, Steve Newman, Casey Wallerstein and Amy Sowers-Wyckoff. Thanks also to the 'fantastic five' who conducted the interviews and wrote material for the book: Abbie Bernstein (From Page to Screen, Ioan Gruffudd), Bryan Cairns (Jessica Alba, Chris Evans, Kerry Washington, John Ottman), Tara DiLullo (From Page to Screen, Michael Chiklis, A Day in the Life of The Thing, Filming) Anthony Ferrante (Creating the Effects) and David Grove (Julian McMahon, Production Design, Costume Design). Plus, thanks to David Hughes for helping out. A big thank you to Stan 'The Man' Lee for his introduction, and last but not least, to the entire cast and crew of *Fantastic Four*, for their enthusiastic cooperation with the project.

Did you enjoy this book? We love to hear from our readers. Please e-mail us at: **readerfeedback@titanemail.com** or write to Reader Feedback at the above address. To subscribe to our regular newsletter for up-to-the-minute news, great offers and competitions, email: titan-news@titanemail.com

Visit our website: www.titanbooks.com

A CIP catalogue record for this title is available from the British Library.

Printed and bound in the USA.

FANTASTIC 4
THE MAKING OF THE MOVIE

Introduction by Stan Lee

Abbie Bernstein, Bryan Cairns, Tara DiLullo,
Anthony Ferrante and David Grove

Screenplay written by
Mark Frost and Michael France

TITAN BOOKS

CONTENTS

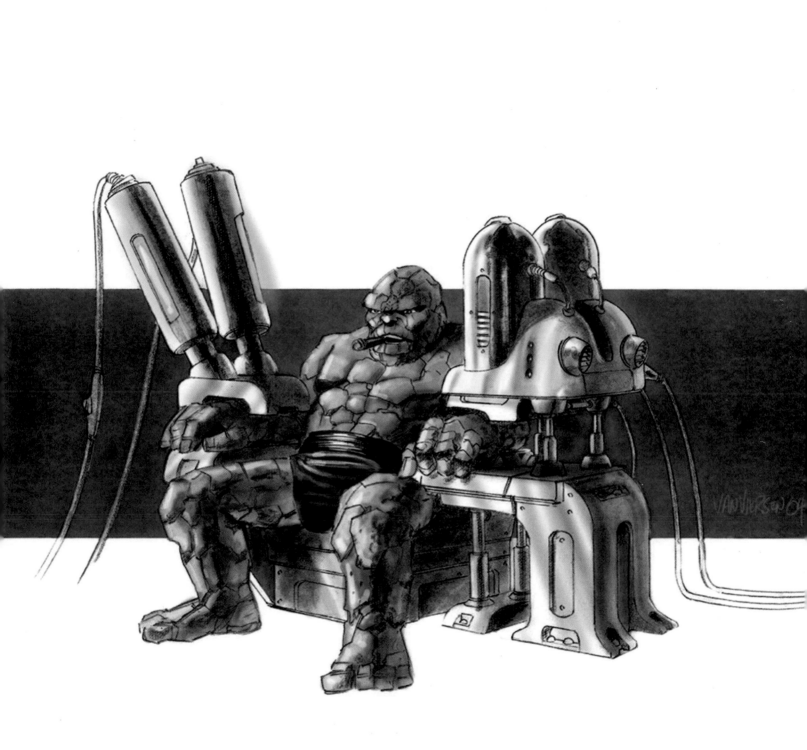

INTRODUCTION

By STAN LEE

You can never predict what'll happen! When I first created the Fantastic Four I expected that my publisher would fire me on the spot. You see, it violated almost all the 'Rules of Superherodom'. For one thing, the heroes had no colorful costumes. Also, they had no secret identities. In addition, for the first time in any comic book, the heroine was the sister of one of the heroes and another of the heroes would soon marry her, so three of the four would eventually be in the same family. Finally, one of the heroes was arguably the ugliest guy in comics. So you see, even at the outset, the F.F. was not your typical comic book team.

I love breaking the rules. So, the next thing I tried to do was create the world's worst villain, good ol' Dr. Doom, but I made him someone who couldn't be arrested. Why not? Because I crowned him King of Latveria. Naturally, as a king, when he traveled abroad he had diplomatic immunity.

Another thing you may not have noticed. Doc Doom has one overriding ambition. He wants to rule the world. Think about that a moment. You could tell any lawman in any country that you want to rule the world and there's nothing he can do about it. You see, if you check your law books, wanting to rule the world isn't listed as a crime anywhere that I know of.

So the world's worst villain can't be arrested and technically isn't even a criminal.

By the way, I'm truly proud of the name Latveria. It sounds so authentic that people are always asking me how I got permission to use the name of a real country. But of course it isn't a real country; I made it up. Hey, if I ever lose my job, maybe I can become a country namer.

Well, getting back to never predicting what'll happen, I never expected the F.F. would one day be featured in a huge, big-budget, blockbuster motion picture.

Didja know I was asked to make a cameo appearance in it? Naturally, there was no way I'd refuse. But I do have disappointing news for you. Believe it or not, I wasn't given one of the starring roles. It was obviously an oversight on the director's part, but I ended up playing Willie Lumpkin, the mailman. However, if any of

you are able to vote when Academy Awards time rolls around, be sure you spell my name right.

It sure was exciting to be on the set while the movie was being filmed. The actors were brilliant, the director was terrific and the crew seemed to be enjoying it as much as I was. But I've gotta tell you about the ever-lovin' blue-eyed Thing, played by my good friend Michael Chiklis. I never dreamed any human being could really manage to play The Thing. I always thought he would have to be a computer-generated image. But Michael brought Aunt Petunia's favorite nephew to life better than I ever thought possible.

In fact, I'll go out on a limb and make a prediction. Last year, the best-selling costume for children's parties was Spider-Man. This year, I'm willing to bet that The Thing's costume will outsell everything else in the stores. I know, when you see the movie, you'll agree with me.

Well, the world's greatest superhero quartet has traveled a long road since its start in the early sixties. But I think you'll agree — it was well worth the trip.

Excelsior!

Stan

Above: The Thing makes his entrance in *Fantastic Four* issue 1.

Opposite top: Jack Kirby's original comicbook frame is recreated for the movie.

Opposite bottom: Stan Lee on set with director Tim Story.

IT'S CLOBBERIN' TIME

PUTTING THE MOVIE TOGETHER

In the beginning of the Marvel Comics universe, there was Stan Lee, and he was great. Lee is responsible for creating many of Marvel's icons. Amongst the most enduring of these is a team that ranks as one of Lee's favorites — the Fantastic Four, which he and legendary artist Jack Kirby developed together.

Lee says the genesis of the Four came about when Marvel publisher Martin Goodman became aware of National Comics' (later DC Comics) *Justice League* series: "He said to me, 'Why don't we get a group of superheroes and try that also?' So that was the spur. I tried of course to make the Fantastic Four totally different than the Justice League, the only similarity being that it was a group of superheroes, rather than just a single one."

And so were born the genius scientist Reed Richards, aka the super elastic Mr. Fantastic; Sue Storm, the force field-wielding Invisible Woman; her brother Johnny Storm, the hot-headed Human Torch; and Ben Grimm, the rock-hard lump of bad attitude known as The Thing. Beginning with November 1961's *Fantastic Four* issue 1 — which told the now classic origin story, in which the Four travel into space for a fateful, transforming encounter with some cosmic rays — the team quickly became Marvel's First Family, their adventures enjoyed by generations of fans in hundreds of issues. Over the decades, they've faced countless adversaries, but one man has become their ultimate nemesis: Victor Von Doom, aka the masked megalomaniac from Latveria, Dr. Doom.

Flash forward to the 1990s, by which time Marvel was

This spread: From issue 1. The new superheroes begin to discover their powers.

Following spread: An updated origin story. Early pre-production art of the space station scene.

branching out into the film business. *Fantastic Four* producer Avi Arad says that after some false starts, efforts by Marvel and Twentieth Century Fox to develop the new film began back in 1994 or 1995. "There were different takes, different writers," Arad recalls. "We had some scripts that were just too big to really do anything affordable with. As time went by and different studio executives got involved, technology changed, and made it possible to do." Back in the mid-90s, the CGI (computer-generated imagery) techniques that allow Reed Richards to stretch, or Johnny Storm to blaze without burning up, simply did not exist. But even now, with state-of-the-art effects, Arad notes that in the Fantastic Four and Dr. Doom, "You have five characters that are pretty complicated, both from a CG and interaction standpoint.

"What works so well in the Fantastic Four," Arad continues, "is that it's a dysfunctional family. The interrelationship of the family is what makes the movie attractive. All of them have the same issue: can whatever happened to them actually end their lives the way they know it? Developing the movie, it took a long time to find the balance between the action/adventure and the character interaction. So we had many, many scripts, many rewrites." Arad says neither Marvel nor Fox rushed the development process: "We always felt that

this particular franchise — it's like the old Gallo commercial, 'Don't serve before its time,'" he laughs.

Over a period of years, several writers did script drafts, but it was in the hands of *Hulk* screenwriter Michael France that the right origin story began to evolve. "I've wanted to see a big screen Fantastic Four movie since I was a kid, reading a stack of the comics in the back seat of the car on long trips," says France. "Taking a swing at a Fantastic Four movie is one of the reasons I wanted to get into movies in the first place." Getting the tone of the script right was a key concern. "The tone direction was to follow the original comics," France recalls, "though that was more an agreement than a direction. I wouldn't do it any other way. We wanted to keep the adaptation thrilling and full of things you'd never seen in a movie, particularly in the use of their powers, but also to keep it funny, because that was a big part of the comics too. Nothing campy, just situational or character humor, like Johnny and Ben constantly fighting like kids... kids who could accidentally destroy half a skyscraper!"

After several other drafts, writer Mark Frost (*Twin Peaks*), also a huge fan of the comics, stepped in to continue shaping the script. "I was a collector when I was a kid, so I knew the stories intimately," Frost says. "When

Right and far right:
The Fantastic Four
assemble, as written
by Stan Lee and
drawn by Jack Kirby
in 1961's issue 1.

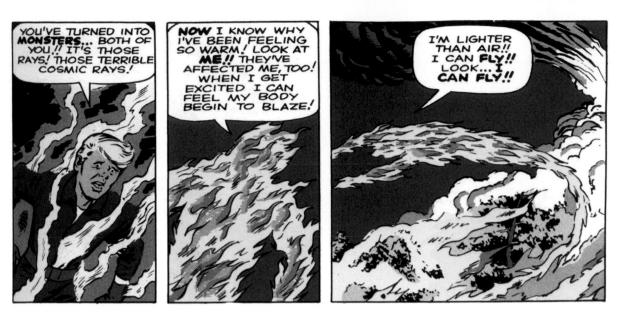

I met Avi about it, I felt the script needed to go right back to the roots of the comic. They had gone off in a lot of new high-science directions, but I felt that at its core, the story was really very simple. My instinct was also that this needed to be an action comedy. It was one of the earlier Stan Lee/Jack Kirby collaborations, and it had a bubbly feel to it. I wanted to get that feeling into the movie; I felt that was something a modern audience would really want to go along on the ride for. You had to have fun with this movie; it wasn't a dark movie like *Hulk*. This wasn't the *sturm und drang* of Peter Parker, or the angst of Bruce Banner. With the exception of Ben Grimm's tragic storyline, which does have comedic elements, this is a lighter experience, and almost a screwball comedy on one level."

The script also needed to capture the excitement of the team gaining their powers, while introducing a whole new audience to their mythology. "We had to update the facts of the origin," Frost says. "They couldn't just be going up into space in a little test rocket like in the comic. We made it a much more elaborate space station. The thing that they encounter in space needed to be something a little bit grander than just a random belt of cosmic radiation. I found a way to compress all that. You want to get going on a story like this: the fun of the story is seeing them transform and watching them come into their powers, and their shock and surprise at what's happening to them. That's the thrill I think the audience is looking for, in terms of recognition and remembering what was cool about the comic."

Screenwriter Simon Kinberg (*XXX State of the Union, Mr. and Mrs. Smith*), who came in after Frost to continue work on the script as the shoot approached, agrees that the comic was important in anchoring the focus of the screen story. "You try to be as loyal as humanly possible to the essence of the characters," says Kinberg. "There are nearly fifty years of the comics, which means there are thousands of stories. You can't be true to the stories, just the characters. We tried to build the movie around the characters — and then you can go to town. Any plot

that feels like it could come from those characters means you go in that direction. Tone is very important. I talked a lot to Fox and Marvel about this, because the X-Men movies are actually tonally easier to write than this movie. It's a lot easier to be serious than funny. The *Fantastic Four* comic is even bright visually, so the movie

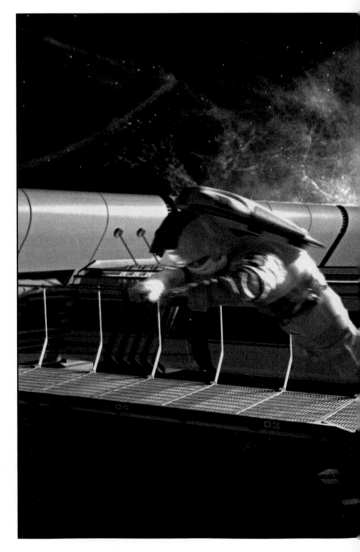

has to be bright and fun. The way to make sure the fun doesn't become silly and goofy is to ground the characters in something real, to make sure the emotions are real. For us, our guide was to be true to the characters, the essence of the tone of the comic, and build a story that services those things. It's a little like doing a biopic about real people. You have to be true to who the person was, but the episodes and scenes may not have actually been taken directly from their life."

At the time Kinberg was hired, he says, "They had a script that had a lot of good stuff, but needed reshaping. It was a much more plot-driven script. The first act of

Left: The cosmic storm, from 1961 comicbook panel to 2005 movie frame.

Following spread: Early pre-production art. An unmasked adversary gazes across the city at the Baxter Building.

the movie was always the first act of the origin story from the comic. They go up into space, the radioactive thing happens, and they come back down and realize they have strange mutations and powers. In a lot of the drafts that preceded mine, the second act of the movie had the Four with their powers, and now they are superheroes — stopping bank robberies and rescuing little kids. It felt like it wasn't a human response to that transformation. I felt like the strength of the comic book is the conflict among the Fantastic Four, rather than between them and some outside force. It's what I thought would be specific and different about this franchise."

One of Kinberg's biggest priorities was to bring more humanity into the latter sections of the script. "One of the things the comic books did really well was to humanize the characters, so you feel they are normal people. What I was really strident about when I came on board was that the second act needs to be about them dealing with the fact that they've transformed. If any of us woke up and we could suddenly become invisible, or catch on fire, or stretch, or we'd become a huge rock-like creature, we'd all have a different emotional response to that. Our first impulse would *not* be to go fight crime, if we weren't cops," Kinberg laughs. "They were scientists and pilots, so it was all about differentiating their responses to this event. The Thing's response was obvious, because he is the only one who can't turn his powers on and off. He's always this grotesque creature. For Reed, because he is a scientist, it was always about looking at himself and the others as specimens. For Johnny, it's his chance to be a rock star and have groupies. For Sue, it became less about being a mother figure, like in the comics, and more about her being the friend we all knew in high school that kept everyone together."

Another great challenge for the script was Dr. Doom. While Doom is a full-out villain in the comics, the early script drafts had trouble integrating him into the lives of the Four. Mark Frost elaborates, "We needed to give them a history with each other that created a story which allowed you to get the conflict and drama that you need with an origin movie. Victor Von Doom needed to be someone that they already knew. He had to be someone that Reed had history with and, more importantly, someone that Sue had history with on a romantic level. That created a three-way tension between them, which helped set up the drama to come."

Finding the perfect balance for Doom proved very difficult, so the character received intense script attention. Director Tim Story explains, "When I got the script, I found that the Fantastic Four characters were actually very well thought out and put together. The thing that all of the writers, and myself, didn't have a handle on was Dr. Doom. The villain wasn't 100 percent, and that means we hadn't taken full advantage of his potential. This is a villain that everybody else has taken little bits of and built their villains around over the years (when you look at Darth Vader, he's pretty much Dr. Doom). He is one of the all-time greatest villains, and we

Right: Dr. Doom made his comicbook debut in issue 5, and is still battling the Fantastic Four today, decades later.

had to make sure he was represented like he was supposed to be in this movie. He is the engine for the storyline — it's his jealousy, and need to be the best and most powerful guy around that moves it along. Like they say, most movies are only as good as their villains, so we had to do right with Dr. Doom."

"We also did a lot of work on the third act of the script during the production," Kinberg elaborates. "I was really focusing on refining and defining Doom's character. Figuring out his agenda, his emotional response to the Fantastic Four's celebrity, and playing the love triangle between him, Sue and Reed without *over*playing it. It's a delicate balance, because not done right, it can be awful. We had to make it as personal as possible, so the third act of the movie isn't — like it was in an early draft — about Dr. Doom and his army of nanobots trying to take over the United States from his castle in Latveria. Maybe you can do that in a third movie, but this first movie is about Doom wanting Sue, Reed getting in his way, and his empire and ego crumbling. Doom wants to eliminate the cause of those problems, and that feels emotional, rich, identifiable and real. He's just trying to take them out, and make Reed feel like *he* feels. Doom is the wayward son. They can't control him, and they've got to learn to give up on him."

Kinberg also helped smooth out the action sequences with director Story. "The big thing that Tim and I worked on," Kinberg says, "was trying to make sure that action sequences were about character. The conflict, the jeopardy and the action of any major set piece had to be an expression of character. If I have any specialty in these kinds of movies, it's finding ways for

action to work as metaphor. Every sequence needs to be exploring, exposing or deepening the character arc. For instance, the second act bank robbery changed into a scene about The Thing and Johnny fighting in the street, because The Thing wants to stay undercover and Johnny wants to be a movie star. We kept doing that to all the set pieces. The strength of those sequences is that you don't know who is going to win. If the team is just going to stop a bank robbery in the middle of a movie, you know the bank robbers are going to jail. If you have two of your heroes fighting on the street and the other two heroes trying to stop them from fighting, you don't know how it's going to resolve, and it does have repercussions for the rest of the film. Audiences are so savvy with these

Above: Filming in Reed's Lab.

Below: Director Tim Story prepares a scene.

Following spread: Pre-production art from an early draft of the script, which included scenes of an escape pod from the space station crash-landing back on Earth.

multi-million-dollar movies with CGI that if you just give them empty action, they will fall asleep. There is nothing big enough for them any more. So we needed to be creative."

"The last draft we had, we said, 'Yup, this is going to be a fun movie to make,'" Avi Arad recalls, "'because the characters are very well-developed, CGI caught up to us over the years, and we can dramatize the characters and make the movie we hope will be fun to see.'"

Executive producer Kevin Feige, who joined the Marvel team in 2000 after working with them at Fox as a producer on *X-Men*, relates how the studio and producers came to agree on Tim Story as the right director for *Fantastic Four*: "Tim had done *Barbershop*, a movie that we at Marvel were big fans of. There were a lot of characters in that film — it wasn't a big action spectacular, and yet it was equal parts hilarious and endearing, which is not an easy combination to come across. You liked these characters, and you also felt that they were *real* characters, not caricatures. So when we heard Tim was a big fan of this comic series — he knows almost every issue inside and out — we just couldn't wait to meet with him. We sat down around a table here at Marvel Studios and had a great time talking about how he envisioned these characters, how he envisioned the palette of the film. It really connected with how we had been thinking of the film for years. He didn't come in and describe, 'Well, the spaceship's going to gleam like this when it comes off the cosmic cloud…' He came in and talked about the four people as if they were four real people. By the way, the space shuttle and the space station are incredibly spectacular," Feige adds with a laugh, "because he wouldn't settle for anything less, but he had a deep understanding of the core issue of who these four characters are, and how they interact with each other."

Story laughs when talking about getting the job. "When I met with [*Fantastic Four* executive producer] Ralph Winter, who also produced *Planet of the Apes*, *X-Men* and *X2*, I knew that if this guy is behind the movie, there

would be no problem. I knew he was going to use the people he's used on everything else he's done, so I had a head start, because he was going to surround me with the right people. That was what brought me into a place of confidence and thinking I could do it. Yet even learning this action stuff, I found out that at the end of the day, it's all storytelling. If your action doesn't encompass the character arc, then it really is just a bunch of stuff blowing up. I had to get into the action of it all, and figure out what was going to tell the story. If they are saving somebody, what are the stakes in them saving somebody? So I really got into how the action was going to complement the character arc, as well as how I was going to physically film it."

Because the characters are so iconic, assembling the right group of actors was even more essential than on most productions. "I must admit, it was a hard movie to cast," Story observes. "We didn't want to just throw in every obvious movie star that you read on Internet lists! You don't want people to sit there and go, 'Hey, that's so-and-so playing blah-blah-blah.' We want them to say, 'That's Reed Richards' or 'That's Ben Grimm'. We went for the best people possible, and it took a long time; we

SIX SPHERES ORBIT THE POD WHEN ACTIVATED
CREATING AN ELECTRO MAGNETIC FIELD AND ALLOWING DNA REVERSION TO OCCUR

FANTASTIC FOUR
REVERSION CHAMBER - ENERGY FIELD
WARREN FLANAGAN '04

Above: Tim Story and Michael Chiklis discuss a scene.

went through *so* many people! Finally, it came down to the five we found. I really don't believe anybody else could have played the parts as well as they did."

With the director and cast in place, the movie entered the final stages of pre-production, leading up to the Summer/Fall 2004 shoot in the city that has in recent years been jokingly dubbed 'Hollywood North': Vancouver, Canada.

It was time to make the final choices as to what the look and feel of the movie would be, and as always, inspiration was taken from the original source: the Stan Lee/Jack Kirby comic books. Associate producer David Gorder, who was part of the team poring over the comics to research both story elements and production design, remembers a particularly key decision: "In the original Kirby drawings, The Thing was smaller, and the rocks making up his skin weren't so defined. Later in the comics he became much bigger, and he towered above the other members of the Fantastic Four. But we had to figure out what works cinematically — do you want a giant character? We liked a lot of the Kirby elements, so The Thing in the movie is smaller in stature than in the later, post-Kirby comics."

As well as taking up residence at Mammoth Studios (home to the largest soundstage in North America), the production also filmed in the heart of Vancouver. A key location was the building used for the Fantastic Four's base, the Baxter Building. It is a kind of character in itself, executive producer Ralph Winter observes: "The structure in Vancouver that serves as the Baxter Building is an historical landmark. It's called the Marine

Building and it's one of the foremost examples of Art Deco architecture in the Pacific Northwest. So we had to be very careful while filming in the lobby, and other places we used there for the exterior. We actually duplicated their elevator, so we could use it in our interior set, which we built in the studio across town."

Winter, who was hands-on with the day-to-day aspects of production (Feige describes him as "the general on the battlefield"), says that the most challenging scene to pull off was probably the major action sequence that takes place on the Brooklyn Bridge — which actually was all shot on a specially built set in a Vancouver parking lot. "We knew it would be difficult, because it takes place during the daytime," Winter admits. "A lot of times, we set special effects sequences at night, to hide what you don't want to see! Daytime composite shots [where special effects and the background are added in post-production] are expensive, and when you're on a bridge, you can see *everywhere*." Adding the background is not a simple job when it surrounds the set 360 degrees, and is even 'below' it!

Avi Arad notes that the bridge sequence serves a dramatic function, as well as being an action highlight: "On the bridge, they're not a team yet. That was very consciously designed, that really only one of them is effective, the rest are still fumbling. The last scene in the movie is when they all realize that together, united they stand."

Though the water in the bridge scene was added later, another sequence featured plenty of 100 percent real water on set, as The Thing and Dr. Doom find themselves being swept through a flooded corridor during

their climactic fight. "We filled up some of those large cargo containers," Ralph Winter reveals, "dropped our two stunt boys inside and then flushed it down the hallway, capturing the water at the other end so it didn't flood the stage. Then we had to recycle the water for take two! The special effects guys, headed by Mike Vezina, calculated what kind of pressure it was going to take, so that we could build the set properly. It all worked like a charm."

David Gorder points out that the production team's love of the Fantastic Four shows up even in the small details on screen, one of which is a sly nod to another Marvel/Twentieth Century Fox film franchise: *X-Men*. "In Victor Von Doom's office, he has pictures of himself posing with various famous people," Gorder notes. "We decided that it would be fun to show Victor with President McKenna and Brian Cox as William Stryker in the Oval Office. We got a photo from *X2*, took Senator Kelly out of the picture, and inserted Victor Von Doom. So the fans who are familiar with *X2* will think that's great — 'Oh, there are some classic Marvel villains, Dr. Doom and Stryker, shaking hands.'"

Gorder is also the man responsible for liaising between Marvel, Fox, and the toy and gaming companies developing *Fantastic Four* tie-ins. "On comic book movies, work on toys and games begins when the movie does," he reveals. "All of these corporate partners need tremendous lead-in time so they can get their lines into production and out in time for the release of the film. Cyber-scanning is a big part of that, which is a digital scan of each actor in character. The companies use that data to create toys and videogame images. Usually, the scanning happens as soon as the actors are cast, or a prosthetic make-up is finalised."

After the principal shoot wrapped just before Christmas 2004, the film moved into post-production. How long did the filmmakers have? "Not long enough," Ralph Winter laughs. "About twenty-two or twenty-three weeks."

Post-production is when many of the Four's powers are put onto film via the wonders of CGI, Winter explains. For example, with Johnny Storm, "We decided early on we would never try to use a stunt person with real fire. It's just never going to be consistent — it was never going to create the kind of cinematic look that we wanted. The trick is to tailor that effect to who that character is — it's not simply that his exterior is on fire, it's that the heat emanates from *inside* of him."

What about the Invisible Woman? "For Sue, we tried to come up with an invisibility effect that you could trace a dotted line back to *Predator*, but updated a little bit."

Reed Richards' stretching abilities required a combination of prosthetics and CGI effects, Winters adds. "We played with some prosthetics where the stretching is minor, so we can do some of that with a fake hand or arm inside of a uniform, but ninety-five percent of that effect is in the computer because the stretching, particularly with the skin, needs hair, muscles and bone structure — and that is better handled by the computer."

Nevertheless, Kevin Feige says his favorite moments are not the big effects sequences, but rather, "Whenever you got the four of them together. When you walk onto the set and you see Reed Richards and Sue Storm and Johnny Storm and The Thing together and you go, 'Holy mackerel, we're actually bringing the Fantastic Four to life!'"

Above: Filming Stan Lee's cameo appearance as mailman Willie Lumpkin.

A FANTASTIC CAST

MEET THE STARS

MR. FANTASTIC

IOAN GRUFFUDD

An actor since the age of eleven, Ioan Gruffudd (pronounced Yo-wan Griffith) has played all sorts of parts, starting as a schoolboy in the Welsh-language soap opera *Pobol y Cwm* and moving on to a career which includes such highlights as a British officer in the mega-hit *Titanic*, a dog lover in *102 Dalmatians*, a U.S. Marine in *Black Hawk Down*, Lancelot in *King Arthur* and the nautical hero of the award-winning TV series *Hornblower*.

The obvious bad pun is irresistible: is playing the book-

ish nature of *Fantastic Four*'s scientist Reed Richards, aka Mr. Fantastic, a bit of a… stretch? Not really, says Gruffudd: "I likened Reed's journey to Horatio Hornblower's journey. Hornblower's a boy becoming a man, and Reed Richards is a brilliant man gaining his social skills and his social confidence as the movie progresses, to become the leader of the Fantastic Four."

On the other hand, Gruffudd says depicting Reed's elastic superpowers "was probably the hardest bit of acting I've had to do, because it was such a visually technical shoot. All the stretching became rather frustrating, because I could not physically do it — I'd have to imagine it. There's a shot in the trailer of my arm stretching beneath a door and opening it from the other side. On set, that was all done with me just imagining. What I thought they might do was to use a close-up of my own arm opening the door, but in fact, what they have done, in order to make the shot look more real and more impressive, is put my whole arm in digitally. So what you saw was me behind the glass window, and then just my eyes looking up as though I was trying to unlock the door. They put the arm in afterwards. There was a lot of that during the movie — me imagining the rest of my torso spreading across a street for example, or my arms stretching, protecting the crowds."

Gruffudd's first contact with the Marvel universe was reading the *Fantastic Four* screenplay prior to his audition. However, once he was cast as Reed, he says, "I went back to the beginning, really, and I got the collections of the early comic books. It was great to discover that we were touching upon the original version in our film. It's a bit updated, obviously, with special effects and spacecraft, but the essence of it remains the same — how we become the Fantastic Four and the relationships that we have in the movie were there in the beginning, so I was pleasantly surprised."

Some of the scenes found Gruffudd performing physical feats he'd never done before, like acting while suspended by a harness. "There was one scene I did with Michael Chiklis," Gruffudd explains enthusiastically, "where The Thing and Reed Richards have a fight, and The Thing throws him the length of his lab. I was on a harness, and I shot at an angle up towards the sky and then swung back towards him, as if I had stretched entirely and then sprung back at him."

Gruffudd describes the harness rig as "an elasticated one. You pulled it back so it was taut, and then on a given cue, they would release it and I would catapult forwards." A stuntman usually does this sort of work, but

the filmmakers felt it was important to see Gruffudd as Reed in the shot. "They said it was perfectly safe and, 'We'd love you to do this.' And I was game for it. I saw the stuntman demonstrate it a couple of times, so it was all set up very safely. Those boys are so professional and so good that the risk factor is minimal. It was fun!"

One of Gruffudd's favorite sequences is the brawl between Mr. Fantastic and The Thing in Reed's lab, which called for a different type of stunt work. "I'm physically on his back, grappling with him, and he's walking around, slamming me into things, trying to shake me off," the actor explains. It's a stuntman in The Thing suit when Gruffudd launches himself onto Ben Grimm's back, but, as Gruffudd reveals, "For the close quarters fighting, it would be me on Michael's back. I would *gently* place myself on his back. Michael was carrying sixty pounds of costume and wearing those big shoes as well, so we all had to be incredibly careful not to pull any muscle or to overburden him."

The filmmakers took care not to injure Gruffudd, either: "We put a pad on my back, specifically for that beat of when The Thing is slamming me against things. They would film a 'hard' slam with the stunt guy on another stunt guy's back. But if there were close-up shots, we would almost be placing me onto the edge of whatever I was being slammed against and then I would sling my head backward, so there was never any real physical pain or damage done."

Wearing Mr. Fantastic's signature blue spandex outfit was something of a stunt in itself, Gruffudd relates. "I think we all look after ourselves as actors physically, and you have to have a certain amount of fitness just to get through a normal shoot, let alone a physical shoot like this one. But I had a little bit of help from the costume department. They had built muscle suits to go underneath the spandex, just to enhance the pecs and the arms a little bit. Once it was on, it made you stand in a very heroic, confident manner, so I quite liked it! But it did have that feeling of you fighting against it the whole time, because you're not able to stretch or move as freely. So it was sort of like a mini Pilates workout every day!"

Of course, some of Gruffudd's co-stars were in even more extreme outfits. "The first time I saw Michael in his Thing costume," Gruffudd recalls, "he looked a *totally* different character. It's extraordinary. Although you do see his face in the features of The Thing, suddenly, it was like working with another actor."

Gruffudd channeled his real-life reaction into how Reed feels in the scene: "There's a real connection there — as I'm talking to him, I'm really trying to find the person I know in this new person, and I think that's what happens in the story. And every time Reed looks at Ben, he realizes, 'I've turned my best friend into this thing.' There is a sense of guilt that is played."

Rather than appearance, *lack* of appearance was something Gruffudd had to deal with in some of Reed's love scenes with Jessica Alba's Sue Storm in her invisible

phase. "There were many instances of 'air-kissing,'" he laughs. He's speaking literally. "I would be leaning over to kiss the air after turning to put my hand on her face and then caressing and cuddling with her. And she wasn't there! So we had many a scene where the crew would be in stitches whilst I was making a fool of myself. But because we're all generous with each other, Jessica was always there, just off-camera, feeding me lines, so at least I had something to work off."

Playing a supporting role in *Titanic* whetted Gruffudd's desire to play a lead in a big-budget movie. "A lot of us British actors who were playing officers in that movie would often be in the background of a scene between Kate Winslet and Leo DiCaprio. We blinked in the background," he laughs.

Being cast as Reed Richards in *Fantastic Four* "was a real thrill, because I remembered when I was on *Titanic* thinking, 'Wow, I'd love to be doing what Kate and Leo are doing.' I couldn't wait to get an opportunity to be 'out front' on a big movie like this. I had a little bit of experience of that on *King Arthur*, being surrounded by all those great actors and having a lot of screen time. So coming to *Fantastic Four*, I'd gained my confidence."

Taking Reed from shy scientist to assured leader was a challenge. "I do hope that I've managed to get that journey in there," Gruffudd says. "That was quite tough, because at the start he isn't the leader, he isn't the cool one, he isn't the show-off at all. He's the opposite of that, and it was hard just to trust that by the payoff at the end of the movie, when he *does* become the leader, you'll have seen a complete arc of the character. So if there's a sequel, I'm looking forward to seeing how he goes from there."

As for now, Gruffudd says of playing Reed Richards, "I'm just incredibly excited and quite proud of the fact that a British actor has been asked to play an American character, one of Marvel's comic book icons."

THE THING

Most kids who fantasize about becoming a superhero picture themselves spinning webs as Spider-Man, or busting heads as Wolverine. It's pretty rare to hear anybody aspire to being Ben Grimm, aka The Thing — unless you're actor Michael Chiklis. A *Fantastic Four* comics fan from way back, he shared an early connection with the hero in an orange rock-monster body. "I remember when I was about fifteen or sixteen years old, I said to my older brother Peter, 'If they ever make this into a movie, I really want to play Ben Grimm.' I felt an affinity for the role as far back as then, which is kind of odd," he chuckles.

It's funny how things have a way of turning out, because Chiklis' dogged determination to become a professional actor created the path that eventually led to his coveted role. For almost twenty years, Chiklis has been working on stage and screen making his reputation as a stellar character actor, playing parts like comedian Jim Belushi in *Wired* and Commissioner Tony Scali in *The Commish*. But it wasn't until his current award-winning

role as Detective Vic Mackey on *The Shield* that Chiklis became more of a name in Hollywood, and caught the attention of many people, including Marvel President and CEO Avi Arad. "Believe it or not, I went to a *GQ* magazine party about two years ago, and my agent Greg Siegel introduced me to Avi Arad," Chiklis recounts. "I knew exactly who he was, and my first words to him were, 'Avi, I have two words for you... Ben Grimm.' He sort of looked at me like, 'Huh?' We hung out that night, but then I put it out of my mind. Six months later, I got a call from Avi's office saying that he wanted to meet with me. I had an inkling as to what it was about, because I had been reading in the trade press that they were gearing up to do *Fantastic Four*. Sure enough, Avi said, 'Michael, I've looked into the eyes of Ben Grimm!' It was lovely of him to say that. It got the ball rolling, and the rest is history."

Twenty years on, Chiklis found himself in the slightly surreal position of getting exactly what he had wished for as a teenager. Yet before agreeing to take the part, he still wanted to make sure that the production was going to do justice to the comic book icons, as well as bring The Thing to life in a way that would work on all levels. "My very first discussion with Avi, and later director Tim Story, was about how to make The Thing come alive, and then it was all about character, and the relationships between the characters. I also told them, 'If you are going to do this CGI, then I am much less interested in doing it.' Of course, I ended up almost kicking myself for saying that, because the suit was such an incredibly uncomfortable experience," he sighs. "But Avi was very clear to tell me, 'Oh, you are going to love Tim. He totally understands the characters.' I love Avi, and think he is a *mensch* of a guy and incredible to work for and with, so I trusted him."

Chiklis says subsequently meeting Tim Story sealed the deal for him in deciding to take the part. "We both recognized Ben Grimm's character as being the heart and soul of this film. He's an everyman that people will be able to relate to and connect to. My opinion, as an artist, was that if you are going to make *Fantastic Four*, you have to make it accessible to all audiences. You have to focus and get the family nature of the film. The Thing is the curmudgeon, and there is this brother-like banter between him and Johnny Storm, where they are constantly badgering each other. Ben has a true affection for Sue Storm, and wariness about the love triangle between her, Victor Von Doom and Reed Richards. My worry going into the room for the meeting with Tim was that

it would be a conversation purely about the technical aspect of making the character physically work, and there would be no time spent on the person Ben is. Nothing could be further from the truth, and by the time I left the room, I called my wife Michelle and said, 'I want it! Tim understands it, and gets it.'

"The script is also so well conceived and well written," Chiklis continues. "The thing that makes so many Marvel comics so accessible to audiences is that they are almost classical Greek drama, thematically. They are built with broad, epic themes: good versus evil, love triumphant, and man's inhumanity to man. They are very ancient, tried and true themes, but set in modern days, with cool powers! You add those elements and you have the making of something really amazing." Chiklis reasons that The Thing fits in with those epic themes by being the literal and figurative 'rock' at the center of the film. "The whole film revolves around his dilemma. He is the only one [of the Fantastic Four] who has been physically transformed in a permanent way. He views himself as monstrous. The others have been endowed with these wonderful, unique powers, but essentially they are still themselves. They can function normally without invoking them if they don't need them. One has

to wonder, why you would want to go back? With Ben, he just wants to be Ben again. We wanted to make it so the audience completely understood that this has utterly ruined this man's whole life. It's cost him dearly from the get-go. His fiancée's first reaction is to scream in terror and run from him — rejecting him completely. It's heartbreaking.

"Everyone stares at him, and all of a sudden he is a freak," Chiklis continues. "He's not a guy that likes to call attention to himself in the first place. Now all of a sudden, he has all this attention on him, and initially it's all negative. Then he starts to realize his strength, and through the arc of the story, he starts to see where he could be very valuable to humanity with these powers. There's a very selfless quality to this character, and that's probably the biggest reason why I wanted to do it. At the end of the picture, there is a moment that really was the thing that completely made me go, 'OK, this is a great character to play!' When he's been transformed back to his former self and he realizes he can't help as a normal man, he then selflessly realizes he has to forget about himself — and go back to being The Thing. It's a truly heroic moment. It's a beautiful thing to be able to play a real hero — a hero's hero. From playing an anti-

hero, like Vic Mackey, to a real hero is a lot of fun. There's no gray ambiguity with Ben Grimm. He's a hero through and through."

Aside from the great character development, Chiklis says the sheer scope of the production completely blew him away, and took the experience to yet another level. "The morning I walked onto the set of the Brooklyn Bridge scene was a little overwhelming for me. It took my breath away to see that massive set. It goes under the legend of, 'You know you are in a big movie when…' I walked onto that set and it was too big to be on a sound-stage. It was a big section of the Brooklyn Bridge they built with a half a mile circular track running through it, so they could run traffic on it. The whole thing was then cased in three stories of blue screen so later on they could put in New York. This was big movie making! All of a sudden I was a fifteen year-old kid living out a dream fulfillment," he says with awe.

Chiklis admits another personal highlight was finally uttering The Thing's trademark catchphrase, "It's clobberin' time", for the first time on film. "I didn't realize how to heart I would take it. I ended up doing a lot of takes of it. I wanted to get it right, and I wanted to give Tim a number of different choices. It's such a fan favorite and that's when you really feel the responsibility of the character when you are playing an icon. You want to get that right, so it gives people goose bumps when they hear it. There were a couple of takes when we knew it wouldn't work, so as uncomfortable as I was in that suit, that was one time where *I* was the one going, 'Nope, let's go again!'" he chuckles. "I think fans are going to be happy."

The actor hopes that his own satisfaction with the film will end up being shared by the fans, both old and new. "I kept saying to Tim that the people who are the original faithful will really love this movie. It has a lot of the neat, cool *Fantastic Four* moments. All the original elements are there, and it's an origin story. I know some

people will have comments about things, like the brow on The Thing. It's certainly pronounced in the costume, but it's not that over-pronounced, sort of ledge feature [from the comics]. His body was also sort of blob-ish in certain comic book manifestations. Those changes in the movie were deliberate. It's not like these guys couldn't have achieved any look they wanted to get. These are incredibly talented sculptors that made this suit. We all agreed that if you are going to do it, it has to be in a way that makes The Thing come to life, and really lends an element to make him more human, while remaining true to the original character. I want fans to know that it was deliberate, and there wasn't anything that didn't go through a painstaking process of choices and that wasn't thoroughly sussed out. We all felt this was the way to go. Boy, am I glad we did.

"When I saw that first fifteen minutes cut together, I was convinced it was the human manifestation of The Thing. And in the end, I think we really made a good film."

INVISIBLE WOMAN

JESSICA ALBA

A few years back, Jessica Alba starred as the genetically enhanced scrapper Max in James Cameron's futuristic TV series *Dark Angel*. Now the actress is slipping into tight blue spandex to once again fight for humanity as Susan Storm, aka the Invisible Woman, in *Fantastic Four*. On paper, Susan and Max may appear to have graduated with the same superhero pedigree, but according to Alba, that's not the case.

"No, they are completely different," she says. "In *Dark Angel*, I played a reluctant heroine. Well, I guess Sue is sort of a reluctant heroine too, but Max was kick ass! Every day she was riding motorcycles, jumping off buildings, and fighting people ten times her size. Sue is not a fighter by nature. She's passive, very cerebral, and maternal. Max was very selfish and brooding. If anything, Max was more like a combination of Ben Grimm and Johnny Storm!"

Though she's now well versed in the Fantastic Four's rich mythology, prior to signing on, Alba was unaware of the group or their adventures. To prepare for the role, she delved into a stack of comic books and boned up on their universe and histories. As it turns out, the material only reinforced what drew her to Sue's character. "She was sophisticated, smart, and maternal," offers Alba. "Those three characteristics really popped out for me. I don't get an opportunity to play any of those things very often, so I just thought it would be fun to explore a different side of my personality, and do something different."

As an origin story, the movie lays the groundwork by introducing Sue, her brother Johnny, scientist Reed Richards, college bud Ben Grimm, and successful businessman Victor Von Doom. Similar to Spider-Man and Hulk, these heroes and villains are made, not born. When the five embark on a mission into space, an accident permanently transforms their lives, and eventually pits four against one.

"They go up to study a cosmic storm that basically pulls apart DNA and puts it back together," explains Alba. "They are hoping that by studying this storm, it could possibly lead to the cure for cancer, AIDS, and any disease that lies in the DNA. What ends up happening is the cosmic storm hits their space station, takes apart all *their* DNA, and puts it back together."

Their new-found abilities are derived from their own personalities. For Sue, that means her insecurities. "Sue Storm constantly feels men overlook her. She has to work extra hard to be taken seriously and be viewed as an intelligent person, so she often feels 'invisible'. Most of the time, she ends up outsmarting everyone and seeing the big

picture. Maybe that's where the all-encompassing force fields come from, I don't know.

"Michael Chiklis' character Ben Grimm is quite physical, and is quite a strong arm, so he becomes the most extreme version of that," Alba continues. "Reed Richards is constantly spreading himself too thin. He never gets anything completed. He's a genius, but he's never accomplished one thing completely. He's here, there, and everywhere — so he stretches! Johnny Storm is obviously the very cocky, confident superstar, so he catches on fire and flies around."

Despite the power boost, Sue still suffers from self-doubts, especially about being the only female in the group. "I think she feels it is an 'all boys' club. But at the end of the day, she keeps everyone together," says Alba. "They sort of lean on her. It's a family."

Although adapted from the comic books, the movie introduces new twists to the characters' relationships, particularly by setting up a love triangle between Reed, Sue, and Victor Von Doom. In the film, Sue has actually given up on the brainy Reed and hooked up with Victor. "Well, Von Doom is every woman's dream," says Alba about his appeal. "He's beautiful, charismatic, and caring. Sue is the head of the space department at Von Doom Industries, and he takes her very seriously, not only as a woman but also as a scientist. He gives her a lot of control and power. He treats her really well, and listens to her. I think Reed didn't do any of that in their previous relationship! He was trying to teach her, and when he wasn't doing that, Reed was caught up in his own world. It was like she wasn't even there, because he was so busy. You get to see all that rela-

tionship stuff in the movie."

When Sue's affections move back towards Reed, a jealous, driven Victor goes over the edge. As a result of their space jaunt, Victor has gained his own special abilities, which he uses to wreak revenge against his rival Reed Richards and the rest of the Fantastic Four. But despite his dastardly deeds, Sue has trouble accepting him as a threat. "She has a big heart, so she always thinks positively, tries to make the most of a situation and think the best of people," explains Alba. "Sue gives Victor the benefit of the doubt until the very last minute."

With her impenetrable force fields capable of both offense and defense, the Invisible Woman is one of the quartet's heavy hitters. Indeed, during one memorable confrontation in the pages of the *Fantastic Four* comic book, Dr. Doom conceded that Sue could possibly be the most powerful member of the team. "Yeah, well she is!" confirms the actress. "I am definitely going to agree with that. She kicks butt, but she's subtle," Alba adds. "She doesn't put it in your face. Sue is not a show-off with her abilities." Show-off or not, one scene in the movie has Sue standing up against Dr. Doom's deadly electric barrage, while another has the Invisible Woman containing her brother as he goes supernova.

However, when asked whether Sue saves the day at the film's climax, Alba maintains it is a team effort. "It's Sue to a degree, but it's not *just* me though," she explains. "It is everybody. We all come together. The cosmic storm pulled us all apart, and we all went in our separate directions. It is like any family that deals with a tragedy. There is anxiety, sadness, and a loss of identity. But then we come

together, and really bond as a family unit. Once we realize we're a family, that's when we defeat the baddie. That is what's so great about Tim Story: he's amazing at putting that across on screen. That's why they hired him. Special effects can be great, but if you don't have real characters with real relationships, no one is going to give a hoot how cool it looks."

In an ensemble cast, standing out and grabbing the spotlight can be difficult. So does Alba fret when her character turns invisible and she's not on screen? "No, I get paid the same," she laughs. "It just means I don't have to do all the physical stuff." Too bad her fellow actors can't joke about the same. While Chiklis endured hours of make-up hell as The Thing, and co-stars Chris Evans and Ioan Gruffudd logged in plenty of time in front of the green screen as the Human Torch and Mr. Fantastic, Alba's technical challenge was pulling off her vanishing act.

"It wasn't so much green screen for me as much as it was camera tricks," says Alba. "I'd shoot a scene where I go invisible, and then the next day we had to shoot the scene exactly the same way, repeating all the close-ups, the over the shoulder shots, but without me there. It was the other actor acting by himself. And then they would have to shoot me without the other actor, so they could eventually put it all together to show me appearing and disappearing. It was actually quite draining because I had to help the

actor get to the same emotional place he was the day before. It was thirteen hours of doing the exact same emotions, three days in a row."

Despite plenty of sci-fi elements, and big action sequences such as a Brooklyn Bridge disaster and Dr. Doom raging against the Fantastic Four on the streets of NYC, Alba says she has a particular soft spot for a more dramatic moment in the film. "There is a scene where Reed is testing Sue's powers, and seeing what her body physically does when she goes invisible or projects force fields," reveals Alba. "It is interesting because even though he's testing her powers, she's testing his emotions. It was a really fun scene to play, because he is pure science, and she is pure heart and soul. It's so reflective of their relationship."

Besides standing out in TV series *Dark Angel* and *Flipper*, the California-born actress garnered attention in such feature films as *Never Been Kissed*, *Idle Hands*, and most recently as the lead in *Honey*. Yet even before stepping onto the set of *Fantastic Four*, the naturally black-haired Alba had already dyed her locks for her roles in the movies *Sin City* and *Into the Blue*. So looking back, does the old adage that 'blondes have more fun' ring true?

"I don't know," chuckles Alba. "Maybe. There is definitely a lightness to my personality when I have blonde hair, that's for sure!"

HUMAN TORCH

Prior to landing the role of Johnny Storm, aka the Human Torch, Chris Evans never considered himself a comic book fan. But after getting wind of the script, the star of *The Perfect Score*, *Not Another Teen Movie* and *Cellular* immediately knew he wanted to be involved in such a high caliber superhero flick.

"Well, it was a number of things," says Evans about what attracted him to the project. "First of all, I love comic book movies. They are really big right now and there's been a string of successes, especially from Twentieth Century Fox. Secondly, I love the dynamic of four superheroes. It's really cool when it is not just one person: that team of four is a fun thing to be a part of. It feels more like a family. Of course, it sounded like they were going to get great people to work on it, with great characters. What better superhero to play than Johnny Storm, who is a fun-loving, cocky kind of guy?"

A lot of actors were asking themselves the same question. Many familiar faces were rumoured to be top contenders for the fiery role, but Evans' exuberance, talent, and persistence bowled director Tim Story over.

"I lobbied pretty damn hard for this movie," admits an enthusiastic Evans. "I must have auditioned three or four times and each time, I kind of stuck my foot in my mouth and then begged for a second, third, fourth chance. It was a really big effort on the part of my agents and managers to get me back in there. There were also

a few people at Fox, such as Donna Isaacson, who really championed me, to give me a second opportunity to come back in and give me another try. They really deserve a lot of credit for getting me this far."

The truth is Evans had never even read for any previous superhero material. "I had met with someone about Superman but no real auditions," recalls the Boston native. "I never got an *X-Men* audition. I think at the time it was being produced and was coming together, I wasn't at a

place in my career where I was getting those calls." For Evans, those days are now most definitely over!

In the movie's reimagined version of the Fantastic Four's origin, Johnny is still Susan Storm's younger brother and an integral member of the quartet, but he is also now the pilot of the fateful space flight, despite being fired from NASA's astronaut program by none other than Ben Grimm.

"We're going up into space to study a cosmic cloud of energy that hits us and alters our DNA," explains Evans. "We all come back unknowing at first; we don't realise we have these powers." Their amazing abilities manifest at the most inappropriate times; in Johnny's case, it's during a light-hearted date with a nurse. "The first time Johnny is exposed to his powers is when he's on a mountain snow boarding," reveals Evans. "He goes off a little bit of a jump and bursts into flames without even realising it. At first, it comes as a shock! It's an interesting process getting to know your powers, how to use them, and being comfortable with them."

To the average Joe, the Fantastic Four must seem incredible and somewhat inhuman, but unlike the mutant X-Men, they aren't forced to hide in fear from a public that does not understand their gifts. It's actually quite the opposite: the team quickly obtains celebrity status, and must deal with the pressures of being the world's first superhero family. "We use our powers in public pretty early on," reveals Evans. "The scene on the Brooklyn Bridge pushes us into the spotlight. It's a really different situation to most other superheroes. We don't have secret identities. We're put into the public eye. Of course, Johnny dives right in! He just wants to saturate himself with the whole fame thing. Everyone else is playing it a little more timidly."

Besides bursting into flames, Johnny can generate fire, fly, and raise the temperature. The ultimate expression of those powers is when he turns up the heat so much he goes 'supernova', like an exploding sun. Naturally, such an exhibition is physically draining, and can only be attempted in dire circumstances. And even though the hot-headed Torch is perhaps more likely to be on the offense, he can still pitch in and help with the defense if necessary. "Johnny is of course impervious to flame, and there is one scene where he sees a little girl right next to a car as things are exploding all around," Evans recounts. "So he runs and shields the girl, as a burst of flame climbs up his back. It's a cool moment."

As the movie leads up to the final showdown with Dr. Doom, the Fantastic Four find themselves on a steep learning curve. According to Evans, the good guys receive some serious lumps before figuring out that united they stand and divided they fall. "Well, individually I think we all get our asses kicked," he laughs. "The whole point is to learn to defeat our enemies by working as a team. We are a team, we are a family, and if the family is fighting amongst itself, things are not going to get gone. When we're working together, nothing can stop us."

In terms of costume design, the film steered away from the darker leather threads seen in *X-Men* and *Daredevil*. Instead, taking a cue from the blockbuster *Spider-Man* movies, the costumes remained ultra-faithful to their comic book counterparts, complete with body-hugging blue spandex, black boots, and '4' insignia. To

fans, those trademark outfits may look sleek, but for the actors, they were a bit of a challenge. "Oh man, it was not fun," sighs Evans. "It's definitely a three or four man process to get into those suits: it takes a lot of time!"

To pull off that perfect chiselled body, Evans hit the weights on a regular basis to bulk up: "I wanted to stay in shape. You want any superhero to be capable, so I tried to stay in the gym as much as I could up until when we started shooting, and even throughout the shoot. They did give us muscle suits which are a wonderful perk," says the already muscular Evans, "but my goal is to get to the size where no muscle suit is needed. Then, I will be a happy guy!" In the meantime, Evans and co-star Ioan Gruffudd suffered with the white muscle gear under their costumes. "It really is the muscle suit that made it so difficult and restricting," comments Evans. "The actual Fantastic Four suit is okay, but the muscle suit underneath made it very uncomfortable."

Enduring any discomfort that came with the job was made a lot easier for Evans thanks to the positive atmosphere Tim Story brought to the set. Story may not have helmed a big budget, special effects-heavy movie before, but the actor has nothing but praise for his director. "Tim did wonderfully," says Evans. "Being a good director is not just about having a vision for the film, it is about having the right attitude, and the way you captain a cast and crew. Tim's demeanor and calming presence

trickled down and really made everyone not only happy in the work place, but also made them work harder and more efficiently."

Since Evans, like all the key cast members, has signed on for a sequel, he's already looking forward to what we might see in the second instalment. "I'd want even more action with their powers," he suggests. "The majority of this film is a bit more humanized, with them trying to get used to their abilities, finding comfort with being superheroes, and understanding their new roles in society." A sequel, Evans thinks, could let rip with even more "real bad ass, ass-kicking fight sequences." The group has such a diverse rogues' gallery, from planet-eating Galactus to evil counter-parts The Frightful Four, so which Fantastic Four foe, or foes, would Evans like to burn next? "That's a good question," he says. "I heard Mole Man might be in there, maybe Puppet Master, but I'm not sure. They are keeping it under wraps!"

As production on the movie draws to a close, Evans looks back on his time as Johnny Storm. How to sum up the experience of becoming the hottest man on Earth for six months? "It's been pretty damn cool!" Evans laughs. "What little kid didn't run around pretending to shoot fire, and jump off the couch and imagine flying? Being the Human Torch is a dream come true for my inner child."

DR. DOOM

"I've been a *Fantastic Four* fan since I was a kid!" says Julian McMahon. "And I've always thought of Dr. Doom as being the original comic book villain, who set the bar for every other villain that followed." For the Australian-born actor — best known to TV viewers as Christian Troy in the award-winning drama *Nip/Tuck* — being cast as Doom in the film version of *Fantastic Four* was a double challenge. "What I love about my role in the film is that I actually get to play two different characters: Victor Von Doom and Dr. Doom," he says. "This movie is about the evolution of Doom, and so I get to play Victor, as his body is slowly being transformed, as two people in one. You get to see Victor as a man before he becomes the monster that's Dr. Doom."

In terms of creating the human character of Victor Von Doom, McMahon and director Tim Story made the decision to focus less on his origins in his native country of Latveria and more on the character as he exists today. "Originally, there were going to be scenes set in Latveria, which was thought to be an Eastern European country somewhere between Austria and Bulgaria," McMahon reveals. "But then we decided not to film them, because Tim felt it was better to set the story entirely in the present, especially since all the fans have read the comic books, and know Doom's story. In terms of my voice in the film, Tim and I agreed that I would speak with an Australian-American type accent,

although Von Doom's origins are really more Eastern European. As an actor, my challenge was to try and project Von Doom's back-story, since we don't actually see Latveria in the film. Although Tim and the film's production designer, Bill Boes, created a Latverian flag for Victor's office that looks just like the flag in the comics."

Victor is first introduced in his office at the Von Doom Industries headquarters, a fifty-story monument to Von Doom that includes a thirty-foot statue of its owner in front of the building. "They sculpted me for that, and it was quite amazing to see a statue of myself on the set every day," says McMahon. "I think the statue tells us a lot about Victor; that he wants everyone around him to feel a bit smaller in comparison, that he wants more of everything. The building's also in the shape of a V, which tells us about his ego and self-obsession. Victor's ambitions are limitless. Inside his office, everything is so grand, with ornate furniture and a chair that looks like it was taken from *Dracula*. He's the ultimate alpha male."

McMahon doesn't view Victor Von Doom, the man, as an evil person, but rather as an adventurous businessman with a towering ambition that tends to go too far. "He's not a good man, exactly, but I certainly don't see Victor as a bad man," the actor says. "He believes in charity — or charity as he sees it — and he's also a scientist who very much wants to make the world a better place, at least through his own eyes. He's more about adventure and conquest than money. If he was just about money, why would he have gone with Reed and the others up to the space station? Why would he have taken that risk? He's very manipulative, but the main thing about Victor is that he's not a man who's ever going to talk about his feelings. He's not open about himself. Other than that, I just see him as a highly aggressive entrepreneur who thinks he's making the world a better place."

Even before he becomes Dr. Doom and faces the Fantastic Four, Victor's rival is, of course, Reed Richards. "Reed and Victor went to MIT, and there's a grudging respect between the two men, but also an intense rivalry," McMahon points out. "The difference is that Reed's interests lie with the chemicals and the hard science, while Victor's more of a businessman." There's also a

rivalry when it comes to the affections of Susan Storm, who at the start of the film, seems to be attracted to Von Doom. "No, I think Susan just likes Victor at the beginning of the story because of his money, to be honest," says McMahon with a laugh. "They're both alpha males but Reed, unlike Victor, is more willing to open up about his feelings, which is ultimately why Susan falls in love with Reed. But when Victor transforms into Doom, the loss of Susan is one more thing, along with the potential loss of his company, that drives him insane."

McMahon believes that the audience will feel sympathy for Victor's plight. After all, the events that lead to his monstrous transformation aren't his fault. "It's interesting that the film does have the courage to blame Reed for being wrong about the calculations with the cosmic explosion," McMahon notes. "Victor says to Reed, 'Are you sure you know what you're doing, because this seems like it's wrong.' He questions Reed, and then the cosmic storm hits. Let's face it: Reed screwed up!

"The transformation of Victor into Dr. Doom is slow and methodical and it happens in a very interesting way," the actor continues. "He's struck by metal from the space station. It starts with a cut on his face, a big scar, and it just grows like a virus until Victor becomes

the cut, and vice versa. His body is transforming into indestructible metal." Once back on Earth, Victor finds himself going completely insane, his rage driven not only by his worsening condition, but also by his anger towards Reed. For McMahon, the challenge was to make Victor's evolution into Dr. Doom believable, both emotionally and physically: "The Doom mask is in a glass case in Victor's office, so that's where he gets the mask from. As for Victor's state of mind: he's angry at Reed for screwing up the calculations on the space station, and I don't blame him.

"The toughest part of filming was putting on the prosthetic suit," McMahon recalls. "Especially the prosthetic scars, because even though we were filming in Vancouver in freezing winter, I got very hot, but I couldn't sweat at all because it would ruin the make-up." The discomfort was worth it though. "I *loved* seeing myself as Dr. Doom, the character I read in the comic books as a kid," McMahon enthuses. "In the film, I play him as a character that's very dramatic, who uses a lot of physicality and theatricality. Doom's perfectly suited to the stage, just like Victor is, with that ornate chair he sits on in his office. But Dr. Doom is made of indestructible metal and that changes you, obviously. He can flick his finger and crush cars, or send buses and street lamps hurtling, and he can lift ten tons. The heart of his strength comes from his ability to summon the power of electrical currents from all kinds of sources — computers, televisions, anything with electricity in it. Victor was a man pushed to the brink because of the accident on the space station, and then we see him get pushed *over* the brink. That's when he becomes Dr. Doom."

Victor's main rival for the affections of Susan Storm may have been Reed Richards, but Dr. Doom's main rival, in their battles on the streets of New York City at least, is Ben Grimm, better known as The Thing. "There's a running feud in the film between Victor and Ben because Victor's always getting crap from Ben and he doesn't like it," agrees McMahon. "The only person who was more damaged on the space station than Victor was Ben; Ben and Victor were the most damaged, and that makes them the perfect enemies. The Thing's really the only character, physically, that can match up with Dr. Doom. When Doom discovers Reed's reversion machine, he's so far gone at that point that he sees it more as a tool to defeat Ben, transform The Thing back into Ben Grimm so he can't defeat Doom. He doesn't see it as something that can help him, because it's too late — what was left of Victor is gone."

McMahon has high praise for Tim Story: "Tim has a unique style as a director and I think *Fantastic Four* really is a family film, about the characters," he says. "Tim wanted us to have fun making the film, and he was very open in terms of discussing my character, and listening to my ideas about how the character should be played. I'm happy that Doom's not just a monster in a suit. You get to see Victor, the man, before he's transformed into Dr. Doom, and we see the transformation step by step: we start out with Victor as a charming businessman and then follow him as he becomes the monster. As for my performance, one of the things I'm happiest with is that we got Doom's eyes right: my eyes look good in the mask, which is so important. Dr. Doom's all about the eyes!"

ALICIA MASTERS

When the Fantastic Four head out in public, their presence can't help but attract a lot of attention — and that is the kind of buzz Kerry Washington is becoming accustomed to. The actress, who has appeared in such feature films as *Against the Ropes*, *Save the Last Dance* and *The Human Stain*, hit the jackpot in 2004 by co-starring alongside Jamie Foxx in the Ray Charles biopic *Ray*. Leading up to her role in *Fantastic Four*, she confesses that like some of her cast mates, she was previously unfamiliar with the legacy of Marvel's first superhero family. Then she landed the role of The Thing's beautiful — and blind — girlfriend, Alicia Masters.

"I was aware of the Fantastic Four because I have boy cousins who read it, but I wasn't a huge fan, and didn't have an intricate knowledge of the comic," says Washington. But the actress gained new respect for the comic book genre after watching *X-Men,* and was equally impressed with the people behind it.

"I had heard they were doing *Fantastic Four*, so I called my manager and said 'What's going on with it?'" recalls Washington. "As soon as I saw the first *X-Men* movie, I really wanted to be involved with these producers, who do wonderful, amazing work. Their comic book movies have meaning behind them, and have things to say about life and society, which I feel is so important. My fiancé [and fellow actor] David Moscow has taught me in the last few years how graphic novels are commentaries on the society we live in. And these producers really honor that tradition. So I called to find out what was going on, and heard about the character Alicia Masters. I thought that would be a really good role to fight for."

In the comic books, the character of Alicia Masters is white, and unfortunately, some fans can be close-minded about any alterations. Was this a concern? "I knew it could be a bit of an uphill battle because she has never been an African American," says Washington, "but I felt this would be a great way to update it."

Before beginning production, Washington immersed herself in *Fantastic Four* lore and was thrilled to discover her character's father was actually one of the group's greatest nemeses, The Puppet Master. "I was excited," she exclaims. "And the fact that he's referred to as my stepfather in the movie really opens it up. Anybody could play him in a sequel. I'm really excited to see where we go with that."

In the movie, Alicia initially encounters Ben Grimm

at his favorite bar, but only after he's rocked out from his outer space adventure. The two make a strong connection, which might explain why Ben becomes obsessed with reversing the transformation. "No, I think he wants to be human again simply because he's afraid of change, like we all are," counters Washington. "He's afraid of being this new thing he's turned into. Alicia is one of the people who helps him embrace the change, and know he's still special, no matter what has happened to him on the outside."

As a new couple, Washington notes the two definitely show their affection towards each other. "We don't kiss in this one, but I am signed on for sequels, so we'll see," she says. "We don't kiss, but there is lots of hugging and touching." So what was it like wrapping her arms around the rough-skinned Thing? "It gives me something to do as a blind chick," explains Washington. "His face may not be as smooth as a baby's bottom, but that gives me more as an actress! Because I had to work with my other senses besides sight, the fact that he feels

so strange was really helpful."

Washington did the requisite research into playing a blind person, and she couldn't have asked for a better teacher than her *Ray* co-star Foxx, who received an Academy Award for his performance as the blind musician Ray Charles. An important tip was to stay 'blind' as much as possible, not just when the cameras were rolling. "I would try to rehearse most scenes with a blindfold once or twice," the actress reveals, "so I could figure out what I would be stumbling around."

Washington enjoyed playing Alicia so much, she is already revved up about exploring her character further in a sequel. "Obviously, I'd like to see a lot more Alicia Masters, and some kissing!" she laughs. "I want the challenge of trying to kiss a prosthetic. And I definitely want to meet The Puppet Master. There's a nice relationship between Sue Storm and Alicia in the comic books. They become friends, and I'd like to see that on screen. There's actually sort of a hint of that in the very last scene of this movie."

STRETCH IT TO THE LIMIT

FANTASTIC EFFECTS

Most comic book movies only have to worry about making one superhero icon look extraordinary. When you have four that have to be *Fantastic* — all at the same time — it can definitely be a daunting task.

"One of the biggest challenges with *Fantastic Four* is that you have characters who are doing amazing things, but in a real world atmosphere," explains visual effects producer Kurt Williams. "Very few movies integrate the powers of their characters like we did in a scene. We created each character's powers by using different technologies, but always making sure it looked photo real, like it's within our world."

The film also had to make sure that the focus was on the characters' performance first and foremost, without the effects trickery getting in the way. "Most comic movies haven't had to deal with creating extensions to their characters that are seamless," says Williams. "It's not like the Fantastic Four change shape into some sort of creature and that's when the computer generated imagery begins. We had to make sure we captured a performance: the CG needed to be an extension of the actors. For example, in one scene you'll see Reed as a normal man and in another scene his arm is stretched out, but you have to feel at all times that you're seeing *one* character, integrated with his or her individual powers."

This philosophy worked in tandem with the approach director Tim Story wanted to take. Many visual effects movies in the past would film actors primarily against a green screen (or blue screen) for all the effects work, but Williams agreed with Story that it was more important to let the actors perform their scenes live on set. Only later would Williams and his team figure out how to add the CG elements.

"It's not like we can do a changeover and go to a solely CG character. The CG is integrated into the live action performance," says Williams. "We really gave Tim the ability to have his actors on set and let it be an ensemble. We let them interact the way they would interact naturally, and then applied their powers to them. That way, we got their true character, and didn't step off into a CG world that called attention to itself."

With over 900 FX shots, seven visual effects companies (three of them working solely on the characters themselves) and a litany of research and development, all of the CG effects nevertheless had to fit together seamlessly when the characters inhabited the same scene, even though different companies handled the effects for each of their powers.

"We had to get all the facilities to really work together, and create a technical hierarchy where they built the shots so they all looked as if they were done by one facility," says Williams, who also worked with special make-up effects supervisor Mike Elizalde to ensure Marvel's first dysfunctional family looked suitably fantastic. "Often times when they use multiple facilities, it looks like a different movie from scene to scene, and every character looks different. So my approach to the film was one character per facility. Whoever got the character had to check their egos at the door. Every supervisor from every facility consulted with each other. We created a very open platform to determine what the effects looked like, and how they all integrated together in the finished film."

A REAL STRETCH

MR. FANTASTIC

Of all the F.F. heroes, Reed Richards, aka Mr. Fantastic, was the most problematic for the visual effects artists, since there had been very few attempts to create a photo real stretchy man on the big screen.

"As a character, his powers are newest to an audience," says Kurt Williams. "When we went to pull references from other movies for the character, we didn't find much for Reed, so in a way we had to build him from the ground up. Often when stretching was done in the past, the conceit was blown because the effect looked too animated, or it was not used correctly in action, so it 'broke the rules of physics' in a way that audiences couldn't understand or relate to."

As with most iconic comic book characters, Williams

Below: Reed is caught in the cosmic storm.

Opposite: Mr. Fantastic in action, as visualised by the film's concept artists.

felt it was important to stay true to the imagery that fans would expect, whilst also ensuring it would look great in a real world setting. "One of the things that happens in the comic books is that Mr. Fantastic tends to look very tubular, and there is not a lot of anatomical detail in him," he notes. "In order to create real world physics that people can 'buy' on screen, we needed to stay true to his anatomical build, which is to say the musculature."

Early on, Williams and his FX team did a test to see how far they could stretch Mr. Fantastic, so to speak, which gave them a better understanding of where they needed to take the character. "We did a quick arm test and torso stretch, and one of the things we got out of that was we couldn't take great liberties with how he stretches," Williams explains. "We not only had to keep Reed organic, but as is the case with stunts, you needed to make the audience *believe* he's there. So that meant keeping the details of his skin, staying true to anatomical structure and even dealing with minor things like pinch points on the skin."

The finished technique also had to accommodate shooting the performance live on set. "For instance, when Reed's arm is stretching, we let the actor play that on set, and act like he's stretching his arm," says Williams. "Then we had to remove his live action arm, and then replace in some cases fifty percent of his body with CG." But it was worth the effort: "Having actors on set and allowing them to have their chemistry really allowed for the integration of the acting and the FX in the movie."

The final Mr. Fantastic stretch shots were created by Soho Effects, led by supervisors Allan Magled and Berj Bannayan. They began by first building the Reed character into the computer. "They built a CG model of Mr. Fantastic, and developed software that allowed them to stretch any part of his body," reveals Williams. "As he stretches, portions of his body 'regenerate', allowing for the stretch. This regeneration is not apparent to the audience, but is a physical necessity for the effect. This allows us to stretch him, shrink him or add to his form.

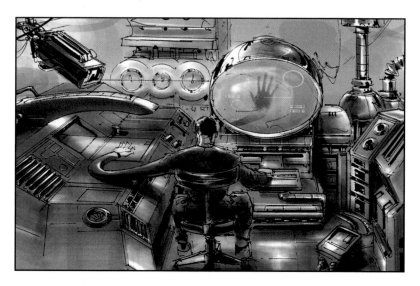

This spread: Reed uses his powers for the first time, from storyboard to final frame.

We can make him as thick or thin as we choose."

In order to finish a given shot, Soho used various layers put together to create an animation with the required photo real effect. "This included his muscle system, bones, joints and skin, as well as surface layers to make either his skin or suit look real when it stretches," says Williams. "When Soho stretched Reed's skin for instance, we had a 'recipe' of twenty-five layers that represented the final product."

This technique definitely gets a workout early on in the movie when the Four are starting to explore the extent of their powers. This leads to Reed and The Thing getting into a fight, which was inspired by images straight out of an issue of the *Ultimate Fantastic Four* comic.

"We needed to figure out how Reed, who is a scientist and not a large guy, was going to fight this big rock man," Williams recalls. "One of the things we decided

was to pay homage to a couple of the comic book frames where Reed wraps around The Thing to constrain him. We started the process on the shooting day, and we shot all this physical integration — your standard fight scene, with the actors — but we took it to the next level in the computer. Reed naturally would outsmart him, so slowly throughout the fight, he wraps The Thing up and constrains him. It's not that The Thing couldn't beat him, but it's a 'buddy' fight. We wanted to let it build up technologically. We started with real actors, replacing in some cases ninety percent of their body parts with CG. But in the end, the action in the scene really fits their characters; it's a good mesh of the characters and technology."

'Cartoony' is certainly something Williams wanted to avoid at all costs with Mr. Fantastic, and the sheer amount of detail needed in any given shot of him usu-

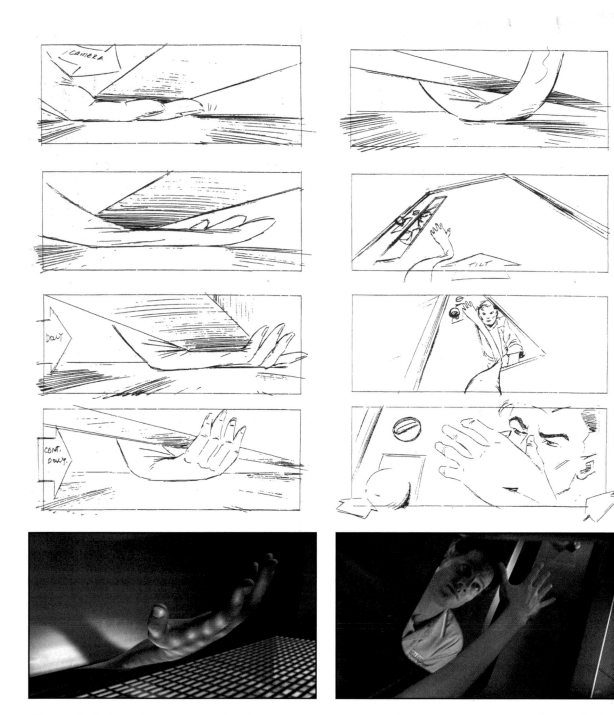

ally required the animators to render about twenty-five different elements per frame to create a realistic stretching effect. "There's a shot early in the film that's about 1,000 frames, so that becomes 25,000 frames that we render for one shot in the movie," Williams notes. "It's very labor-intensive, especially when you have to render simple details you don't even think about, such as cuticles!"

Even late in the post-production process, Reed continued to prove a challenge, as FX shots designed for certain sequences had to be rethought when they didn't work properly. "We had several instances where we would use a particular angle we shot and it looked too animated or rubbery, no matter how photo real it was, or how much of the sinewy texture or musculature we added to him," Williams admits. "The primary thing we did in those situations was go back to a different camera angle, or go to a cutaway and come back to him. It just works better, especially in short glimpses."

One of the biggest modifications occurred during the film's climax, where Mr. Fantastic jumps in front of Sue Storm to save her from Dr. Doom's 'Doom Bolt'. "Reed had his feet planted on the ground and he leaned out, stretched his torso, fanned out and took the hit," Williams explains. "What we found is that the longer he hung out there, it just didn't look right. In order to fix it, we revamped the action so it played more into the momentum of the scene. In a way, it's just like shooting stunts: you have to shoot an actor or stuntman in a particular way to make the event work on film, no matter how extraordinary the event is. So we had to be very careful with how we had Reed stretch in that scene to be effective, and not take the audience out of the movie."

Whereas the other members of the Fantastic Four needed digital augmentation to bring them to life, the creation of the orange-colored Thing took a more traditional route. Michael Elizalde of Spectral Motion handled the formidable task of making Ben Grimm appear rock solid through the magic of special make-up effects appliances.

"One of the biggest concerns we initially had was, 'This guy is made out of rock, how is his face going to move and how do we make it so it doesn't look like rubber?'" recalls Elizalde. "It was important that we make this rock-like surface so the actor could actually emote. It's a challenging assignment, but it's also one of those situations where you know how to structure it. You know where a human face is going to bend, and you know where to put the creases in the rock."

After some testing, the decision was taken to leave the creases and recesses soft. While these were ultimately made out of a low-density foam latex that is very pliable and supple, the rock surfaces were made from a thicker, denser foam latex. "That way when The Thing moved, the areas that were softer gave first, and the areas that were harder retained their shape and looked like rock moving around on the surface," says Elizalde.

While The Thing in the comics has been portrayed as very large and imposing over the years, Elizalde's team (including art supervisor Chet Zar and costume designer Jose Fernandez, who assisted with the art direction) felt it was important to scale him down in size a little, so he would relate better to the other members of the Four, and also to the audience.

The team started with the comic book version of the The Thing and, intriguingly, worked backwards. "The comic book Thing is more of an anecdotal version, or caricature, of the character we ended up designing," explains Elizalde. "If someone saw The Thing down the street, they would say to you, 'This guy is huge, he was made of rock and had a huge brow!', but when you saw the real Thing, you'd realize the description was embellished by this second or even third-hand information. So that's what we did — we were able to pull him back into the world of practical design, so we could make Michael Chiklis into this character, but still have him function and be able to move as an actor. When you look at The Thing in the movie, he's not a giant, he's a person and an individual who is suffering these very horrible circumstances. He's changed from a man to a freak, and we have to be able to see that emotional turmoil. The make-up allowed him to do that."

Opposite: 1,000 pounds of Thing hits the Brooklyn Bridge, from storyboard to screen.

Below: Early concept art. Even a drill doesn't stop The Thing enjoying his popcorn.

During the initial design stage, the face posed the biggest problems. "Everyone liked the proportions, the girth and the width of the body; the only thing we ended up changing was the head," says Elizalde. "The way the head was structured, it looked too much like a cauliflower on top. It was too soft, and not faceted enough. We stayed fairly close to the face in the comics, which gave him a wide lip, pronounced brow and a smaller nose. Very early on in the sculpting stage we actually gave him ears, but we eliminated them. He never had ears in the comic, and the fear was that by having them he would end up looking too much like a Cro-Magnon man."

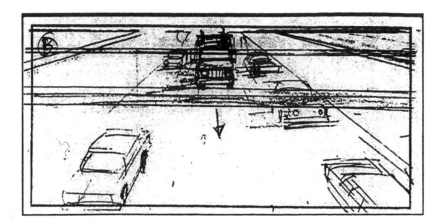

While The Thing is made of rock, Elizalde explains that the story makes clear it's malleable rock, otherwise the character wouldn't be able to move at all! "The rock is pliable to some degree like silly putty, but if you throw it against something, it doesn't deform, it holds its shape," he says. "So he is able to move: the rock actually gives and bends with his movement, but when he runs into something or crashes against something, that's the full force of the rock hitting."

There's another crucial factor that gives The Thing even more 'weight' on screen: Michael Chiklis' performance. "There's only so much you can do with sculpting tools and clay, but to sell it, you have to have a performance, and Chiklis did that for us," Elizalde enthuses. "He made us look so much better with his performance, and his ability to give the character some weight both physically and emotionally. You can't just put anybody in a rubber suit; it's incredibly difficult to pull it off. People don't have any idea how to impart certain emotions and

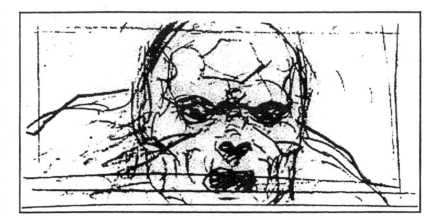

characteristics — very few people have the ability that an actor or physical performer like him has."

As for the application process (executed by Bart Mixon and Jayne Dancose), Chiklis initially spent around three hours in the make-up chair each day to get him ready for the shoot, but by the end of principal photography that time had thankfully been cut in half. "You get a kind of 'muscle memory' down of how to put the appliances on, and it becomes routine," explains Elizalde.

While the rest of the Thing costume is a suit, special over-sized hands were also created, to ensure the character was properly equipped when it came to clobberin' time: "The hands were gloves, where Michael would stick his index and middle finger into the index finger of The Thing's hand, the ring and pinkie would then go into the middle finger, and the thumb would go into thumb. We added a third, prosthetic finger that Michael would control with cables, using his other fingers. The Thing's fingers were about two or three inches longer than normal fingers. It increased the whole girth of the character and made him look proportionally correct."

Although The Thing is nearly 100 percent practical make-up, Kurt Williams reveals that the VFX team also did some enhancements to the character: "Despite Mike's greatest efforts, there were a couple of times where we put The Thing in a situation where the suit just couldn't do it, so we built a CG stunt Thing to help with that."

Williams also used CG to show the force The Thing brings with him as he interacts with his environment. "The Thing jumps off a girder on the Brooklyn Bridge, and when he hits the pavement, we cracked the pavement digitally," he explains. "Those are the kind of things that make a difference. If he's a 1,000-pound character, we needed to treat him that way and show it on screen, but that type of thing is often hard to do physically on set. That's where we tag-teamed with Michael and his group."

Ask Michael Chiklis if he knew what he was getting himself into when he actually *asked* to portray his on-screen alter-ego in prosthetics and make-up, rather than use CGI, and he'll just give you a stern look. In one of those ironic situations where life imitates art, Chiklis was able to intimately experience the frustration and pain of his character, Ben Grimm, by simply donning the suit of The Thing. The actor had no idea how deeply the physical challenges of suiting up as the super-powered rock man would affect him both mentally and physically over the five-month shoot. "I'm not an anxious person," Chiklis admits candidly. "I'm not claustrophobic or a phobic person, but I had a very, very hard reaction the first time I put on the make-up and the suit. It threw me, my own reaction. Trying to intellectually understand what you are getting into is one thing, but when you are actually doing it, it's a very different experience. It's a different world… a different planet!"

Detailing his daily Thing transformation, Chiklis says he showed up in the wee hours of the morning, at least three hours before crew call, to get into make-up. "They used a hospital-grade adhesive that was glued into my nose and up to my eyelids, right up to the eyeball," he explains about the process. "They would put zinc on my lips and glue it inside my mouth. It's very invasive and they can't leave that stuff on you, because it's not good for your skin." Once the face make-up and full-head prosthesis were applied, Chiklis would then have the suit built around him. "I thought it was going to be OK, because I did a life cast where they completely cover your head and face, and there was nothing to it," he recounts. "I was able to stay calm and relaxed. Part of

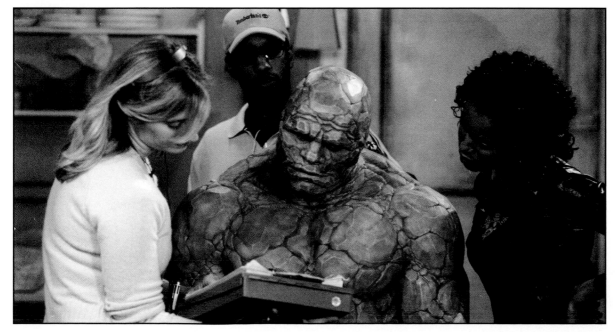

Above left: Concept art for The Thing's 'testing rig'.

Left: Michael Chiklis checks a line.

Following spread: Face to face with Dr. Doom.

Opposite: The
Thing: up close
and personal!

Below: The
make-up team
in action.

it was because I knew I needed to be still for three minutes and that's it. I also had my hands available to me, so I knew if there was any problem, I could reach up and rip it off my face. In the real make-up and suit, the shoes alone were twelve and a half pounds apiece. When they put my hands on, they are really big, and I could only move my hands in a particular way. The tops of my fingers essentially controlled the entire hand. There was no way I could pull anything off of me, including the hands, because they were strapped, buttoned and glued on. When they were on, they were on! Then the most I could carry was a water bottle. That was all I had the strength to hold in my hands, and here I am playing the strongest man in the world! It was very hot and very uncomfortable. All on, the suit weighed sixty pounds."

To help deal with the stress of the daily process, Chiklis consulted a psychiatrist to learn mental therapy exercises. He also relied heavily on the effects crew to get him through the long days. "Thank God, I had my team around me! It was really Michael Elizalde [special make-up effects supervisor] and the team around me that made me let go of my control issues. After a week, I realized there were six people around me at all times. Having them with me, I was eventually able to go, 'Even if I were to black out in this thing, in a matter of minutes they would have me half out of it and help would be on

the way.' They made me much calmer.

"The only times I had a really, really difficult time and I started to feel desperate was when I was in it for more than eleven hours," Chiklis continues. "Once I got past the tenth hour, it started to get very, very hot and I'd start to shake uncontrollably. I think it was just physical exhaustion. There was one day, I went past sixteen hours and I couldn't do it anymore. I reached my personal, physical and emotional threshold. I don't think I've ever been brought to a threshold, where you find out how much you can actually take of something. I was starting to lose motor skills, and that's not something you expect. I will say that I am thrilled that I have a lot of experience as an actor, because quite frankly, the acting was almost a secondary afterthought to everything else. I have a strong foundation in my art and it made things a lot easier. If I had to spend a lot of time focusing on craft, I'd have been in deep trouble," he chuckles.

At the end of the shooting days, Chiklis says the team developed a process to help him detach from the costume: "The biggest clean up was on my face. It didn't take very long to take the actual suit off, maybe fifteen minutes. But every night, we went through a facial. They would thoroughly clean my face and my head, and it would take about an hour, every night. It actually felt really good! I had a massage therapist, and she would rub my feet or hands when I had down time, which helped relax me. It sounds like diva stuff, but it was unbelievably helpful to take me out of my head and frankly, it was company. We would talk, and if I was talking to someone, I wasn't in my head and thinking about the stress." Having endured the process for the duration of the filming, Chiklis admits he's relieved to be out of the suit now. "I learned a lot about myself in the process of making this film. At the end, it ended up being a lovely experience, with a *big* learning curve!"

NOW YOU SEE HER...
INVISIBLE WOMAN

To see or not to see? That is the question when approaching Sue Storm's sudden case of invisibility. "Sue from the beginning is an ethereal character," says Kurt Williams. "The one thing I don't think has really been done in a movie yet is to create a very ethereal version of the invisible woman. She is also a character driven by emotion, so it was very important we related her power to her emotions. She starts off very defensively with her powers, and uses them in a reactive way. Later, she needs to learn to use them offensively."

In other films, Williams notes, filmmakers have tended to take a literal approach to invisibility, but with Sue, they wanted the audience to know Sue was there, even if the other characters didn't. "There's a scene in the first act where Sue's having dinner with Reed, and you see her flicker as she gets emotional and starts to go invisible," says Williams. "At the end of the scene she says, 'Look at me' and she disappears, but we had to deal with the fact that she has clothes on. Our conceit is not that her clothes disappear. Later on she'll learn how to cloak her clothing as well, but in this particular case, we had to create enough detail for you to know it's Jessica Alba."

As with the other characters, Alba was shot live on set to allow for the best performance, with Williams and his animators removing the elements from there.

Above: Pre-production visualistion of Sue's force field in action.

Far left: The cosmic storm hits.

Left: "Look at me!" Sue turns invisible for the first time.

This page: Sue vs. Doom, from storyboard to finished film.

Opposite top: About to disappear... Shooting this scene took many stages, one of which required Ioan Gruffudd to kiss thin air!

Opposite bottom: Concept art of Reed testing Sue's powers.

Stan Winston Digital was in charge of these effects, under the supervision of Randall Rosa and André Bustanoby.

"The challenge was finding a way to shoot her on the set, rather than against a green screen," says Williams. "So Sue's character begins with the performance, usually shot on set. Randall and André built a computer-generated version of Sue, utilizing body and facial scans of Jessica Alba completed by Gentle Giant Studios. They took the performance and essentially replaced Jessica in the shot with the computer-generated version. Then they transition or dissolve from Jessica's real performance to our CG version. This way they matched her performance exactly, and we weren't as reliant on animating her performance from scratch."

The next stage, according to Williams, was mixing the performance and CG model together in a given shot: "All the layers together achieved the effect that best suited the scene. Sometimes she's only partially invisible, and other times she can barely be seen. Our approach with Sue was to make her look as elegant as possible. To that end, we built several CG layers that represented her outline, and edge detail, as well as the inside backs of her clothing."

The animators also devised a way whereby Sue affects her background when she needs to be cloaked. "We compared this to a cuttle fish," reveals Williams. "When the cuttle fish is very still in the water, it takes on the attributes of the background, so when Sue is still, she sometimes disappears like a cuttle fish would. However, the idea is that she's 'projecting' the background or refracting light so you don't see her. When she does move, you will see a little more of her as the background starts to catch up to her."

Sue's fantastic powers also of course include the ability to project a force field. "There's a scene where she fires a force field at Dr. Doom," says Williams. "As you see her get angry, you see the force field formulate — it starts to tug on the background a little bit and there are light shards when she turns invisible, almost an angelic sort of transition. You see it coagulate into something that is obviously coming from her body — it retains her shape — and then it's thrown at Doom. We really wanted it to feel like it's attached to her and she's projecting it."

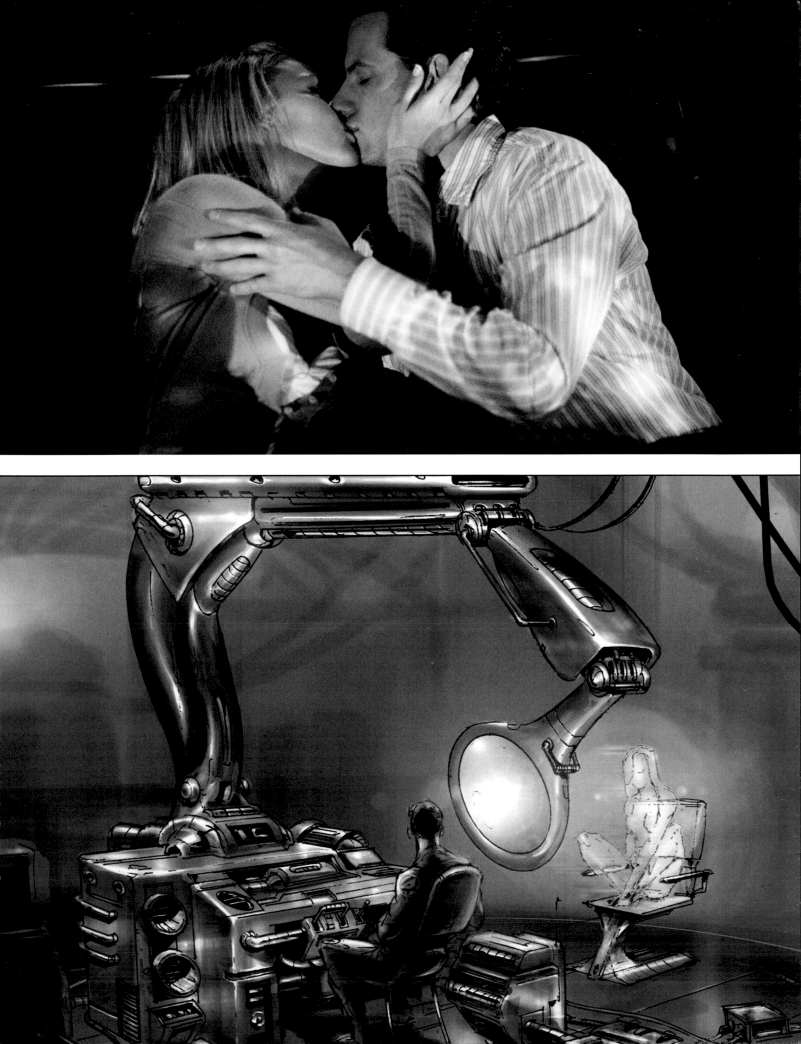

Coming up with answers to Mr. Fantastic's technical issues may have got Kurt Williams and his team out of the digital frying pan, but Johnny Storm threw them back into the fire — literally.

"Fire is one of the most difficult things to do in the computer," Williams admits. "In general, whenever you see the integration of real fire and CG fire in movies, it's always called attention to itself. It's been a point of criticism in a lot of films, and we needed to integrate this character in a scene without him looking like we lit a stuntman on fire."

Creating digital fire has certainly come a long way, but Williams notes that doing it convincingly is still a relatively new breakthrough: "Even three years ago, we wouldn't have been able to create this character the way we created him today. We didn't want to integrate prac-

Right: A life-changing moment.

Opposite: An early concept design for Reed's testing chamber.

Below: Creating digital fire is a real challenge, but Kurt Williams and his team were up to the task.

tical fire on set, or a stuntman on fire, with CG fire. Luckily, digital animation has really advanced, and that allowed us to generate this character while still making it look realistic."

Handling Johnny's VFX needs was Giant Killer Robots (GKR), supervised by Peter Oberdorfer. "I needed an innovative group that could execute all the shots quickly," says Williams. "I also needed someone who could think out of the box. Peter really thought everything through. One of our premises is that Johnny is the *source* of the heat. He's burning 6,000 degrees Kelvin when he's the Human Torch. It's almost like he's a planet on fire. It's a really high frequency heat, because it's so hot at his skin level, you don't really see the skin, or the fire attached to him. There's a lot of energy to it, and where you can see flames, it's almost like solar flares coming off the surface of him.

"It was important that we went back to some of the original comic books for reference," Williams continues. "We realized you almost have to create a negative image. He gets very dark in some cases along the surface of his skin, but his eyes are white and the interior of his mouth is white, so it's like a negative photograph image."

With so much flame and heat on screen, getting the lighting effects right was very important. "You can't underexpose the fire too much because it looks false, like it's been superimposed," explains Williams. "It has to look hot, and have detail and density. That's how it would be with methane gas flame, so we had to expose Johnny correctly against backgrounds. We did as many of his shots as we could at night, because he looks better in darkness, due to the contrast."

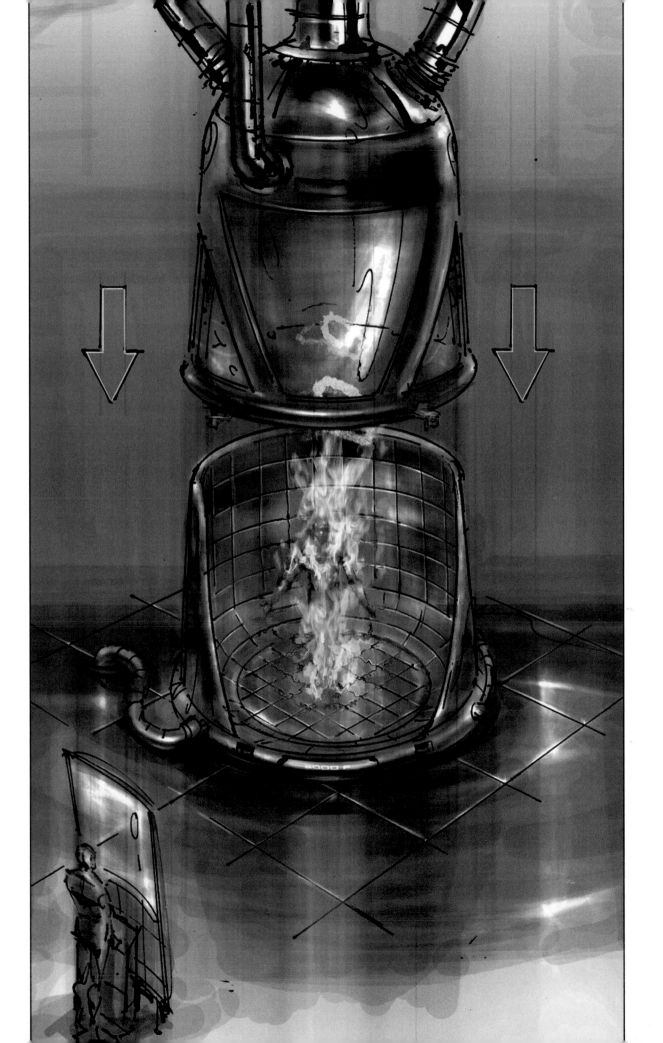

Above: Flame on...
flame off...

Below and opposite:
Pre-production art of
the Human Torch in
action.

In a technique known as interactive lighting, real lights were utilized on set to give the effect that Johnny's flames, no matter how big or small, were glowing, even though the effect on Johnny himself would be added much later. "We used a tremendous amount of interactive lighting," says Williams. "Especially with the big events, the lights barely fit outside of the frame of the camera! And on the small events, we had to work with cinematographer Oliver Wood about how we were going to do the interactive lighting. If it's too strong, then it doesn't look right either. Some of the lighting had to be generated by the visual effects team. So fifty percent is interactive light and the other fifty percent is created in the computer."

GKR started their work on the Human Torch process by building layers that represent his inner core, and then worked outwards. "Most of the layers were built utilizing 'fluid simulations' that allow the elements to interact with Chris Evans' performance of The Torch that was filmed on set," says Williams. "GKR created these simulations and layers in a way that was rendered quickly, and adjusted in the composite. All the layers then react in synch with Chris' movement. Peter built most of these in pieces that allowed us to adjust the flame density, heat signature and all the variables in the composite of each shot. We had to build all these multiple CG layers in a way where it didn't take five months to render a single shot. We would have been in trouble if that were the case!"

Williams is very pleased with the final result. "We created a look for Johnny that has never been seen before," he says. "It will be used as a reference for other characters in future movies."

This spread: Flame all the way on! Johnny takes to the skies.

The Fantastic Four discover who and what they have become early on in the film. Victor Von Doom on the other hand slowly devolves into the villainous Dr. Doom via a series of metallic make-up effects appliances, before finally donning his iconic mask and costume.

"We did some transformational stages for him," explains Spectral Motion's Michael Elizalde. "He starts out with a little cut on his forehead that doesn't look quite right and grows deeper, slowly revealing the metal underneath."

Initially, it was thought that bandaging up the wound during the early stages would be a simple way of Doom hiding his condition, but actor Julian McMahon (who of course is well known for his role as a plastic surgeon on *Nip/Tuck*) had a better idea, that everyone loved. "Julian came up with using surgical staples," says Elizalde. "It's great, because it's a fore-shadowing element, and gives you a little bit of an indication that he likes metal.

"So we used little surgical staples to hold his cuts together, and you see these chrome silver elements going on underneath. We used silver leaf gelatin appli-ances to get that effect, so when the light hits Julian just right, you see this nice kick of metal in his wound."

Eight make-up effects stages in total were created as this wound grows on Doom's face, with the final stage resulting in metal protrusions on his flesh. "We wanted the stages to be subtle," Elizalde recalls. "You don't want to turn him into a monster too early in the

Above: The transformation begins... Using surgical staples was Julian McMahon's idea.

Right: Doom's metallic hands are prepared.

Opposite: The transformation is complete.

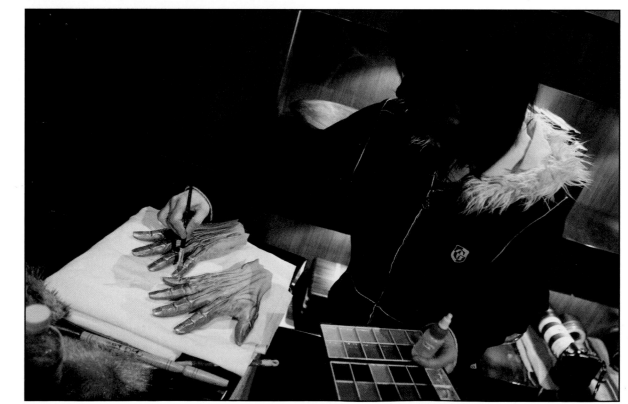

story. This is a very good looking man, so you want to keep him together as long as you can."

Ultimately though, Doom's malady becomes so obvious, he needs to don his costume to hide it from the world. "Stage eight is the last time we see Julian's face," Elizalde notes. "Even when his whole body becomes metal, he still wears the mask, so we don't know what's going on underneath there."

Kurt Williams' team created subtle CG effects to show the physical changes between the different growths on Doom's face. "We show a couple of glimpses of it changing, where you see the metal physically rising to the top of the skin," says Williams. "That way, the audience is going to understand and believe every time he shows up that he's evolving."

The 'Doom Bolt' — where the character harnesses the electrical energy from his environment to unleash a deadly discharge — is another VFX element, also created by Giant Killer Robots, with Peter Oberdorfer and John Vegher supervising.

"Like the other characters, his power is being generated from inside his body," says Williams. "We created the effect so you see some bone structure and vascular qualities, so it doesn't took like it's just shooting off the end of his fingers. It's generated from inside his body, and that enhances this metallic look of his skin."

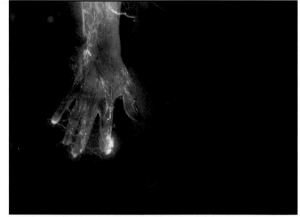

These electrical effects scatter across surfaces, as well as jump from point to point — just as electricity would in reality. "GKR created the software for this effect for other movies, but customized it for Doom," Williams explains. "The requirements for the Doom Bolt itself as generated by the character required an intense, quick-moving look that needed to have more density than the electricity does in reality. We also customized its color into a rich Doom green and blue, which separated it from other effects." According to Williams,

Giant Killer Robots also used interactive lighting on set, to help place the effects seamlessly in the scene.

"Ultimately," Kurt Williams concludes, "the success or failure of these characters that have been created digitally is down to the team of three primary facilities and their supervisors. I need to credit them for our success on the movie. Any time you create VFX that you have never seen before, it requires a collaboration, and I haven't seen a collaboration this successful, on this scale, on any other movie I've worked on."

Above: Attaching the prosthetic hands.

Below and opposite: The devastating 'Doom Bolt' strikes.

THE SCREENPLAY

...AND FURTHER BEHIND
THE SCENES

FADE IN:

CLOSE ON A MASSIVE STEEL HEAD

Our first thought: DR. DOOM? But it's not moving. A welder's torch sparks into frame in the hands of a sculptor on scaffolding. This is art, an epic 20 foot statue going up of a business mogul (VICTOR VON DOOM) in whose generously extended hands sit two intertwined columns of DNA. His face is chiseled, angular, perfect (too perfect). Past sparks, we MOVE down to pick up...

EXT. STREET/VON DOOM INDUSTRIES TOWER - DAY

REED RICHARDS and BEN GRIMM head toward the soaring glass-box atrium of VDI Headquarters. Designed to inspire awe, it does.

REED
High open space, exposed structural elements. Obviously aimed at first time visitors to create feelings of...smallness, inadequacy.

Ben glances at Reed, who looks a little nervous.

BEN
Good thing it ain't workin... Reed, what are we doing here? This guy's fast-food, strip-mall science—

REED
This wasn't our first stop, in case you forgot NASA. And Victor's not that bad. He's just a little...
(seeing the statue)
Larger than life.

INT. VON DOOM INDUSTRIES TOWER - DAY

They move past the statue, into the sprawling atrium.

REED
He's financed some of the biggest breakthroughs of this century.

BEN
You'd never know it.

He motions to a high-tech ORB, showing FOOTAGE of VDI's accomplishments: a safe and clean nuclear facility, the first private Space Station.

All images have VICTOR front and center, glad-handing George Bush, Tony Blair, shady International Leaders. The last image is Victor holding the AMERICA'S CUP.

BEN (CONT'D)
Jesus. That too?

They reach three stern RECEPTIONISTS.

REED
Reed Richards and Ben Grimm to see—

A receptionist cuts him off, handing them each a pass.

SOUND BITES

Julian McMahon
"They sculpted me for the statue of Victor Von Doom that appears in front of Von Doom Industries. The head alone is about three feet tall and I couldn't believe it when I saw it: a thirty-foot statue of myself. It obviously says a lot about Victor and not me. It didn't do much for my ego. I think it's funny."

FEMALE RECEPTIONIST
Executive elevator, top floor.

BEN
What's the price for a smile round here?

They head for the elevator. Reed carries a small, black box. As they enter the elevator, steel doors shut and we CUT TO—

INT. VON DOOM INDUSTRIES TOWER - OFFICE - DAY

A large, dark office. Ben in the corner. He yawns, watches...
BRIGHT HOLOGRAMS: Stars. Planets. They hover in the air, making the room feel like a majestic portal into outer space.

REED (O.S.)
My research suggests that exposure to a high-energy cosmic storm born on solar winds might have triggered the evolution of early planetary life.

REED stands among the holograms, speaking to a MYSTERIOUS FIGURE in shadow behind a desk. An ominous, PULSATING RED CLOUD covers the stars. It washes over a hologram of EARTH.

REED (CONT'D)
In six weeks another cloud with the same elemental profile will pass Earth's orbit. A study in space could advance our knowledge about the structure of the human genome, and help cure countless diseases, extend human life—

The SHADOW clears his throat. Reed speeds up, emotional.

REED (CONT'D)
Give kids the chance to be stronger, healthier, less prone to—

SHADOWED FIGURE
Turn it off. Please.

The figure's DEEP VOICE pierces the darkness.

REED
But I haven't fully explained my—

SHADOWED FIGURE
Yes you have...Imagination. Creativity. Passion. Those were always your trademarks.

Lights brighten, revealing the face behind the voice: VICTOR VON DOOM. 35, handsome,

commanding. He looks almost...airbrushed. He drops a WIRED magazine to the desk. REED is on the cover over the words: RICHARDS BANKRUPT, GRANT CUTBACKS.

VICTOR
But dreams don't pay the bills, do they?
(a condescending smile)
Same old Reed, the hopeless optimist. Still reaching for the stars, with the world on your back.

REED
You remember in school we talked about working together. That's what I was about to explain...

Reed presses the remote. Another hologram appears: A SHUTTLE slowly approaching AN ORBITING SPACE STATION. Both bear the VON DOOM INDUSTRIES logo. Victor smiles, more intrigued.

VICTOR
So it's not my money you want. It's my toys... Tell me: if NASA doesn't trust you, why should I?

Victor is a step ahead. Reed pauses, thrown for a beat. Ben wakes up, suspicious. Victor notices. He notices everything.

VICTOR (CONT'D)
That's my job. To stay a step ahead. To know what other men don't.

Ben gets close to Reed, turning toward the door.

BEN
I can't take this.

REED
(low, quiet)
Ben. This is business. Just work.

A beat. Victor cracks a smile, enjoying the tension. And...

SUE (O.S.)
He's right, Ben.

They turn to see...SUE STORM (demure, stunning) standing in a corner...possibly for the whole presentation. A little cold:

SUE (CONT'D)
It's just business.

VICTOR
I think you both know my Director of Genetic Research, Susan Storm.

BEN
Heya Susie.
(under breath, to Reed)
One more thing he's got.

Sue gracefully walks into the office, only taking her eyes off of Reed to give Ben a warm hug.

SUE
Ben, it's been too long.

She gives Reed a polite handshake. Victor watches carefully. Reed looks uncomfortable in her gaze. A little tongue-tied.

REED
You're, you've, I mean, how have you bee—

SUE
Never better.

Victor sizes them up. He puts a hand on Sue's shoulder.

VICTOR
This isn't going to be a problem, is it?

REED
Not at all.

SUE
Ancient history.

Victor smiles, eyeing Sue.

VICTOR (CONT'D)
Good. Then you're just in time to hear the great Reed Richards ask me for help.
(to Reed)
You know, you made a lot of folks at MIT feel like a junior high science fair. So you'll excuse me if I savor the moment.

Ben tightens. A hard beat. Reed sucks it up.

REED
You back this mission, and I'll sign over a fair percentage of any applications or—

VICTOR
The number's seventy-five. And it's applications and patents.

BEN
What about his first born?

REED
(quiet)
Ben, the money's not important. We could save lives.

Sue gives a thin smile - a flicker of old feelings.

VICTOR
Twenty-five percent of a billion is enough to keep the lights on for a while, isn't it? Maybe even pay off your fourth mortgage on the Baxter Building.

They look at Victor. How does he know all this..?

VICTOR (CONT'D)
Deal..?

Reed looks at Ben, who shakes his head softly no. But Reed...drops a nod. Done. Victor smiles, offers a handshake.

VICTOR (CONT'D)
Well then, to our future. Together.

Victor squeezes. Hard. His other hand on Sue's shoulder.

VICTOR (CONT'D)
Funny how things turn out, isn't it?

REED
Hilarious.

As Reed and Sue lock eyes, Ben watches Victor. Wary.

INT. VICTOR'S OFFICE - MOMENTS LATER – DAY

Director of Communications LEONARD enters, checking files.

VICTOR
If Reed's right, then this little trip will double our stock offering.

LEONARD
And if he's not..?

VICTOR
Reed's always right. Good thing he doesn't always know what he's got...

INT. VON DOOM INDUSTRIES TOWER - ELEVATOR - MOMENTS LATER

Reed and Ben step into the elevator.

BEN
He knew about NASA. What if he made the call to shut us down—

REED
Ben, think about all the people we can help if this works—

BEN
Maybe you should think about helping yourself for once. You always let this guy push you

round—

REED
We got what we wanted. That's <u>enough</u>.

BEN
I know, I know. I'm just worried about what <u>he</u> wants... Speaking of which...

Reed follows Ben's eyes to...SUE. She joins them. Doors shut.

INT. VON DOOM INDUSTRIES STAIR-CASE – CONTINUOUS

SUE
You sure about this, Reed?

He nods, head down. He doesn't want eye contact.

REED
Those solar winds are flaring, but I factored them into my coordinates and—

SUE
I was talking about us. Working together.

Sue holds her eyes on Reed. He is clearly uncomfortable in her gaze. Did the elevator just get smaller?

REED
(thinking, talking fast)
Well, uh, based on our history...you can handle the biogenetics, and I'll focus on the molecular physics. Or, uhm, maybe I should take the

biotech, you work the microscopes, since you have some background in electropho—

SUE
(droll, a little annoyed)
Right. That's exactly what I meant.

She shakes her head - same old Reed. He looks at her - what did he say wrong? Ben smiles, patting Reed on the shoulder.

BEN
Way to not overthink it.
(to Sue)
So when do we leave?

SUE
I'll schedule the launch. Call me in the morning to talk about resources and crew.

She offers a business card. Reed doesn't take it.

REED
I, uh, think I remember the number.

SUE
It's been changed.

Beat. Ben grimaces. Reed takes the card, his eyes down.

REED
As far as crew, I was hoping Ben could pilot the mission—

SUE
Well, he's welcome to ride shotgun, but we

already have a pilot on our payroll. You remember my brother Johnny...

Off Ben's curdling smile, we DISSOLVE TO—

EXT. LAKE LAUNCH FACILITY – DAY

A helicopter shot through trees. We soar over timberland, and find something massive looming on the horizon:
A SPACECRAFT. A sleek take on a space shuttle. Modern tech combined with industrial design that NASA could never afford. The craft's nose is pointed straight up, ready for launch. WORKERS IN JUMPSUITS are scattered around the two-hundred foot tall scaffolding, performing routine checks.

EXT. GANTRY OVERLOOK – DAY

Ben stares up at the craft. A sneer on his face.

BEN
Can't do it. I cannot do it.

REED
External SRBs, orbital system engines. It's just like the shuttles you flew in—

BEN
No. I cannot take orders from that underwear model. That wingnut washed out of NASA for sneaking two Victoria Secret wannabes into a flight simulator.

REED
Youthful high spirits.

They walk toward the base of the scaffolding.

BEN
They crashed it into a wall. A flight *simulator*.

REED
I'm sure he's matured since then.

CLOSE on JOHNNY STORM, leaning over to kiss a hot redhead. PULL BACK TO REVEAL he's riding a MOTORCYCLE, and she's driving a red CORVETTE with license plate: FRANKIE. PICK UP Reed and Ben, watching through binoculars.

REED (CONT'D)
When have I asked you to do something you absolutely said you could not do?

BEN
Five times.

REED
I had it at four.

BEN
This makes five.

INT. LAKE LAUNCH FACILITY LOCKER ROOM – NIGHT

Reed and Ben unpack gear into lockers. Suddenly—

JOHNNY (O.S.)
Captain on the bridge!

Ben goes to attention on reflex: Johnny snaps a picture with a digital camera. Then advances, as Ben realizes who it is...

JOHNNY (CONT'D)
Digital camera: $254. Memory stick: $59. The look on your hard-ass former CO's grill when he finds out he's your junior officer: *priceless*.

Ben eyeballs Johnny, suddenly reaches up as if to grab him. Johnny flinches. But Ben just reaches for Johnny's zipper, adjusts his uniform.

BEN
I can handle the ship. I can even handle Mr. Blonde Ambition. But I don't know if I should be flying or playing Vegas in these suits. Who the hell came up with them?

SUE
Victor did.

Sue enters, wearing her blue, wetsuit-like uniform, carrying a stack of flightsuits. She hands them out to the guys.

SUE (CONT'D)
The synthetics act as a second skin, adapting to your individual needs to—

JOHNNY
Keep the hot side hot, and the cool side cool!

REED
Wow. Fantastic.

Reed stares at Sue in the skintight outfit. She wonders, maybe hopes— is he *actually* checking her out?

REED (CONT'D)
Material made from self-regulating unstable molecules. I've been working on a formula for this.

SUE
Great minds think alike.

VICTOR (O.S.)
Guess some think faster than others.

Victor enters, wearing his custom-tailored flightsuit.

VICTOR (CONT'D)
I hired Armani to design the pattern. These colors will look great on camera.

A DOOR OPENS. Leonard enters, in a sharp suit.

LEONARD
They're ready for you, sir.

VICTOR
Showtime.

EXT. LAKE LAUNCH FACILITY - HALLS – NIGHT

Leonard leads Victor through the halls. Victor checks himself in mirrors as he walks, fixing his hair, his uniform.

LEONARD
Our numbers are through the roof. The IPO's tracking at fifty, sixty share. The bank's five times oversubscribed—

VICTOR
It's not just the money. I could make money in my sleep.

LEONARD
Then what is it?

VICTOR
History, Leonard. History. Everything else is conversation...
(a beat)
How's the other matter?

Leonard pulls out a BOX. Opens it: a TEN KARAT DIAMOND RING.

LEONARD
Harry Winston sends his regards.

They hit a set of big doors. Victor stops and looks into the reflective, metallic surface on the wall. He fixes one last strand of hair. Perfect. Then he opens the door to...

SNAP!SNAP!SNAP! WHIP-PAN a row of CAMERAS snapping shots of—

EXT. LAKE LAUNCH FACILITY – NIGHT

Retrofitted into a makeshift press area. Victor

sits on a platform, with reporters stretched out below him.

VICTOR
Today we stand on the edge of a new frontier. In the furthest depths of outer space...we will find the secrets to inner space. The final key to unlocking our genetic code lies in a cosmic storm...

BEHIND THE ACTION: Reed, Sue, Johnny and Ben walk past. News crews barely notice, passing without even taking a picture. Our "Fantastic Four" are not exactly big news. Not yet.

BEN
Isn't that your speech?

REED
He's made a few changes.

BEN
This is your dream, Reed. You should be the one up there.

REED
Victor's better at these things.

Just past the press area, they see...one woman standing, waiting. This is DEBBIE, Ben's fiancée. And for the first time in the entire film...Ben SMILES. They hug, kissing.

Johnny and Reed watch. Reed glances at Sue, who walks ahead. Debbie slips a photo into Ben's flightsuit. A tender beat.

BEN
I'll be watching over you.

DEBBIE
Just get back soon, or I start looking for a new groom.

Ben looks at the little ENGAGEMENT RING on her finger.

BEN
Soon as I'm back, I'm gonna trade that in for a bigger rock.

DEBBIE
I don't care about rocks, I care about you.
(to Reed)
You bring him back in one piece, or you can forget being Best Man.

Reed nods, smiles. Debbie gives Ben a last kiss. Ben turns to Johnny, who gives a cocky smile.

BEN
What the hell you smiling at? Just keep your mouth shut, and your mind on those SMBs—

JOHNNY
Actually, the engines are SME's. Hydrogenbase, carbon propellant. Couple generations past your last ride.
(at the threshold)
I'm not as dumb as you look.

Ben just glares at Reed. This is going to be a long trip. As they follow after Sue, we CUT

BACK TO—

VICTOR ON STAGE

Mid-speech. Playing behind him is REED'S HOLOGRAM: stars give way to a pulsating red cloud...

VICTOR
Think of a world without genetic flaws - no asthma, allergies, baldness, breast cancer...

Ben and Reed hear the speech. Ben bristles.

BEN
What's wrong with being bald..?

Victor smiles at the crowd, commanding. A true leader.

VICTOR
Darwin discovered evolution. Now we - I - will define it. Only in America could...

The red cloud of cosmic rays wash over the Earth.

VICTOR (V.O.) (CONT'D)
...a little country boy from Latveria build one of the biggest companies in the world, and truly reach the stars. Now if you'll excuse me, history awaits...

On those words, the HOLOGRAM TRANS-FORMS TO...Von Doom's SHUTTLE on the launch pad. BOOM! THRUSTERS FIRE WHITE HOT. Smoke billows across the pad. Ready for take off.

Victor walks past the hologram and exits. His departure perfectly timed with the shuttle LIFTING OFF.

We push in on the shuttle, and follow the ship as it leaves Earth's atmosphere. BOOM — booster rockets fall away and the shuttle fires its thrusters. The hologram transitions to...

A shot of the SPACE STATION high above the Earth. The shuttle enters from the top, lighting up the hologram with engines afire. As the shuttle approaches the station we CUT TO—

EXT. DEEP SPACE - SAME

THE SPACE STATION in the distance, rotating in orbit above Earth. THE SHUTTLE eases in and docks.

INT. SPACE STATION - COMMAND CEN-TER – SAME

Victor and Sue lead the others into the command center.

JOHNNY
(a "dad voice": to Ben)
If you behave, maybe next time daddy'll let you drive.

BEN
Keep talking, there won't be a next time.

Reed is focused on THE EARTH.

SUE
Long way from the projection booth at the Hayden Planetarium, isn't it?

Reed turns towards her — a little stunned that she would bring that up. *It's the first time she's been nice to him so far.* He smiles, gently, hesitantly, always hesitant with Sue.

REED
Yes. Yes it is.

Johnny and Ben exchange a look. Reed keeps looking at the stars, eyes wide, like a little kid.

INT. SPACE STATION - COMMANDCEN-TER/OBSERVATION DECK - SAME

They enter the nerve center of the space station. Victor goes to a computer console on the observation deck below. The windows are closed, so there's nothing to observe.

VICTOR
(to ground; via comm-link)
Leonard, how's the feed?

LEONARD (V.O.)
Recording, sir. We see you perfectly.

Victor glances at a camera mounted into the console.

SUE
We can monitor the cloud's approach and observe the tests from here.

BEN
Is it safe?

REED
The shields on the station should protect us.

BEN
Should?

VICTOR
What's wrong, Ben? Eighty-million-dollars worth of equipment not enough for you?

Ben turns to Victor. A little tension. Reed cuts it:

REED
Let's start loading those samples. Get your suit ready, Ben.

Victor keeps his eyes on Ben.

VICTOR
So you still do all the heavy lifting?

Victor gives a friendly smile, patting Reed.

VICTOR (CONT'D)
Maybe you should have stayed back in the lab. Field work never suited you.

Reed doesn't defend himself. Ben steps up.

BEN
He does the talking, I do the walking. Got it?

Victor holds tight to his smile. He nods, condescending.

VICTOR
Got it. So take a walk, Ben... I'm going to borrow Susan for a second.

REED
Sure.

Ben and Johnny read his eyes, as we CUT TO—

INT. SPACE STATION - AIR LOCK – LATER

Ben preps for a space walk, putting on a helmet and boots. Johnny unloads a set of clear sample boxes off of a cart, each containing a variety of plants.

JOHNNY
Please tell me your dawg's not trying to rekindle things with my sister.

BEN
'Course not. Strictly business.

JOHNNY
Yeah, well, his eyes say different.

BEN
Hey, two hearts got busted last time. Maybe she's not over it either.

JOHNNY
Let's see: you got Victor, stud of the year, more coin than God? Or Reed, the world's dumbest smart guy worth less than a postage stamp. Hmmm, it's a toss-up.

BEN
Put your tiny little mind at ease.

JOHNNY
Don't you wander off, boy.

Johnny steps out of the air-lock and shuts the door. He looks through a small window to see Ben give the thumbs up. THE AIRLOCK DOOR opens, and Ben gracefully steps into space.

INT. SPACE STATION - OBSERVATION DECK - SAME TIME

Sue descends the stairs at Victor's behest. Joins him.

VICTOR
Surprised I agreed to Reed's proposal?

SUE
I understand the *business* reasons.

VICTOR
Well, when you're looking at your future, it never hurts to find closure about the past.

Sue's eyes narrow. What is this about..?

VICTOR (CONT'D)
Susan, every man dreams that he'll meet some woman he can give the world to.

He presses a button and the observation deck's outer windows open up, revealing a spectacular, romantic view of the EARTH.

VICTOR (CONT'D)
In my case, it's not just a metaphor.

While she stares out the window, Victor reaches into a pocket, revealing a RING BOX. Sue looks unsettled.

INT. SPACE STATION - NEARBY
CORRIDOR - SAME TIME

Reed checks data on a work station, set on a wall. The results of his calculations are not what he expected... He sees WIND VELOCITY digits rise. He does a double-take when he sees the readout: EVENT THRESHOLD, T-MINUS 10:00.

REED
No...no...impossible. It's...too fast.

INT. SPACE STATION - OBSERVATION
DECK - SAME TIME

Behind his back, Victor holds the ring box in hand.

VICTOR
You've been with me two years now.

Sue doesn't know where this is going. She treads lightly.

SUE
It's been a good two years, Victor... The

SOUND BITES

Michael Chiklis
"There was one moment when I was playing Ben Grimm and we were all in our space suits in the space station and we all looked at one another and said, 'Hey! We are the Fantastic Four!' We just started laughing about it because it was very, very cool."

company's accomplished so much.

VICTOR
Right, of course, the company... But you see, I've come to realize all the accomplishments in the world mean nothing without someone to share them with—

SUE
Uh, Victor, I hope I haven't done something to make you think...

He pushes on, a man used to getting what he wants.

VICTOR
Sue, I've lived my life unafraid of taking big steps. And this is the biggest step yet. If it helps, think of this as a promotion. A merger of sorts...
(getting closer)
Four little words that can change our lives...

He is about to spring the ring on her. She looks like a deer in headlights. She opens her mouth, and...WHAM! Doors slam open. REED

RUSHES INTO THE ROOM.

REED
The cloud is accelerating!

Victor quickly puts the ring back in his pocket.

REED (CONT'D)
I don't know what happened.

Sue quickly moves to a nearby control panel to verify Reed's claim. Starts punching buttons. Confirms Reed's findings with a nod. Victor hardens, in control.

REED (CONT'D)
We've got minutes until it hits, not hours... Victor, that storm's deadly - the radiation's lethal. We need to abort.

VICTOR
Get a grip. Reed. We didn't come all this way to lose our nerve at the first little glitch. Just close the shields...

REED
Ben's still out there—

VICTOR
So reel him in. But we came here to do a job. So let's do it. Quickly.

EXT. SPACE STATION - MOMENTS
LATER

Ben is carefully arranging SAMPLE BOXES OF PLANTS.

INTO SPACE

Production designer Bill Boes was determined that the film version of *Fantastic Four* have a visual style that echoed the classic comic book vision of the late, great artist Jack Kirby: "I wanted the look of the movie to be based in reality, and to be very contemporary — maybe five to ten years ahead of us — but also to feature the use of the kind of odd, ambiguous forms and shapes that made Jack Kirby's work so classic."

The production designer began his quest in space. "I wanted to be as faithful to Kirby as possible, so I wanted the space scenes to match what happened in the comic book," says Boes, who modeled the movie's shuttle after Kirby's design in the original *Fantastic Four* comics, as well as an early forerunner of the real space shuttle, known as a 'Pogo Plane'. Boes also designed a magnificent concept for the interior of the shuttle (though the scene set inside the ship ultimately wasn't shot). "The interior of the windshield had the look of those 1960s Italian sunglasses," he says. "The shuttle has a race car-like interior with padded walls and not a lot of buttons, like you see in most science fiction films, because I wanted a minimalist look, in keeping with the Jack Kirby tradition: different, but simplistic. There's also a split-level cockpit and a pilot windshield — it's all a nod to the Kirby style."

Boes' minimalist approach to *Fantastic Four*'s production design carried over to the design of the space station. "When I spoke to Tim Story, we agreed we wanted there to be many different shapes in the film, especially with the space station," says Boes. "I looked at toy designs, cylinder shapes, squares, spheres, and we blended all of those shapes into the design of the space sta-

Right: The unused concept design for the shuttle cockpit.

Opposite: The Von Doom Industries shuttle, ready for take-off.

Right: Concept art
of the shuttle in
flight.

Opposite and
opposite bottom
right: Designs for
the space station
interior.

Opposite bottom
left: The final
space station set.

tion. The exterior, not surprisingly given Victor Von Doom's influence, has a V-look that's very prominent. You know who's in charge! It also tells us a lot about Von Doom's ego, and the monster he's destined to become."

As well as using Kirby's work as reference, Boes also studied the space station seen in Stanley Kubrick's 1968 film *2001: A Space Odyssey*. "That film still looks great, not dated at all. Kubrick also kept everything simple, and that's the kind of design I wanted: believable, simplistic, and not silly."

Boes' use of odd forms and shapes extends to the interior design of the station, where the fateful encounter with cosmic rays occurs. "Again, I wanted the inside to have a minimalist look to it," says Boes. "There aren't a lot of buttons and pipes and all the stuff you usually see in a space station. The interior has a round shape to it, with lots of simple forms and shapes and different colors, lots of ambiguous shapes — Kirby shapes. In terms of the different areas of the station, there's the center hub where the characters are supposed to be sealed from the rays during their experiments. Then, when the rays arrive sooner than Reed had calculated, we see the airlock where Johnny and Reed watch Ben float in space, trying to get back inside. That's where we put in an orange rock-like object, a reference to Ben's transformation into The Thing. There's also a survey room located at the bottom of the station, which was created with the help of CGI, where you can view the Earth. We designed that to be kind of like Captain Nemo's observation room on the *Nautilus*."

In terms of establishing a color scheme for the exterior and interior, Boes used the comic books as a guide: "The outer part of the space station is a combination of white, silver and grey, while the inside has a mint-like look to it. We used a lot of mint-blue colors, off-white, true blue, once again in the tradition of Jack Kirby's visuals."

Boes' favorite bit of design for the space station

sequence was for the key moment when the cosmic rays attack Reed Richards and his team, altering their lives forever. "That scene's an example of real simplicity. I looked back at the old comic books and I noticed that Kirby, in that scene, covered the panels in red, like a 'Code Red', whenever something bad happened. It was a favorite technique of Jack Kirby's to paint a scene in red, and it was very effective. So we did a 'Code Red' too — when the cosmic rays attack, everything turns red and then we cut to when the characters are all back on Earth. It's ambiguous, and creates mystery in terms of the audience wondering what has just happened. I think Jack Kirby would have loved that scene!"

Above and right: The design of the survey room was influenced by Captain Nemo's observation room on the *Nautilus*.

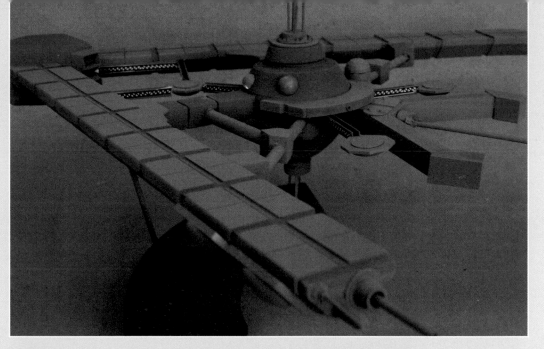

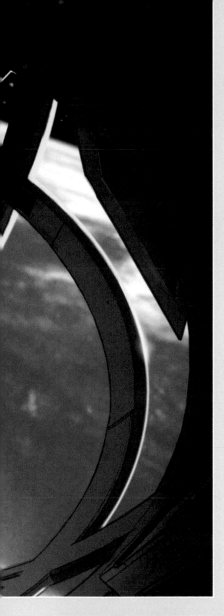

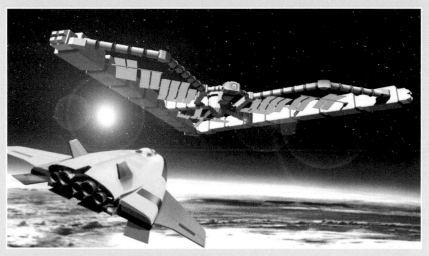

Above: Concept miniature of the V-shaped Von Doom Industries space station.

Left: CG concept art. The shuttle approaches.

Below: A pre-production painting of Ben Grimm on his way to the airlock.

REED (ON RADIO)
Ben, we need you back inside.

Ben turns to see Reed and Johnny staring from a window.

BEN (INTO RADIO)
I ain't done arranging your flowers, egghead.

REED (ON RADIO)
Ben. This is serious. Turn around.

Ben sees Johnny motioning for Ben to look behind him. Ben turns and sees: THE COSMIC STORM, rumbling toward the station. Not close, but not far. That gets Ben's attention.

BEN (INTO RADIO)
Roger that, on my way.

He turns back towards the ship. BEHIND HIM, the storm grows.

INT. SPACE STATION - COMMAND CENTER - SAME TIME

Victor rushes into the room, looks at the monitors. Sees the others near the airlock on one screen, and the approaching cloud on another. Anxiety creeps across his face.

AUTOMATED VOICE
Event threshold in two minutes.

INT. SPACE STATION - AIRLOCK DOOR - SAME TIME

Reed and Johnny stand by the airlock, waiting for Ben. They heard the automated voice. It panics Reed.

REED
Come on, Ben, come on...

VICTOR (ON RADIO)
Reed, we're running out of time.

EXT. OUTER SPACE - MOMENTS LATER

A wake of turbulence from the cloud hits Ben, making it harder to maneuver. The cloud's tendrils snake toward him.

INT. SPACE STATION - AIRLOCK DOOR - SAME TIME

They can see Ben outside the window, still twenty yards away. The entire corridor rumbles. Lights flicker and spark. They watch helplessly.

INT. SPACE STATION - COMMAND CENTER/OBSERVATION DECK – SAME

Sue watches the monitor, also helpless.

SUE
Johnny... Reed...

Victor, annoyed by the indecisiveness, marches right up to Sue. Practically shoves her aside as he hits the INTERCOM.

VICTOR
Reed, you need to get up here so we can close the shields! Now!

Sue glares at Victor. His lack of compassion shocks her.

REED (ON RADIO)
Not until Ben is back inside!

VICTOR
It's too late for him, and soon it'll be too late for all of us.

Victor doesn't bother to wait for a response. He takes over the console, punching keys.

SUE
What are you doing?

VICTOR
Raising the shields.

SUE
You can't leave them out there.

Sue glares with as much contempt as her face can muster.

VICTOR
Watch me. Reed had his chance. You can't help them any more than I can.

Beat. She takes a step toward the door. Not sure what to do.

SUE
I can try.

With one final glare, she bolts from the room.

INT. SPACE STATION - AIRLOCK DOOR - SAME TIME

Reed bites his lip. Thinks. He decides.

REED
Victor's right. Johnny, get to the command center. Close the shields.

JOHNNY
What about you?

One look from Reed tells Johnny, he won't leave without Ben. Johnny eyes Ben, steels his courage. He's not going either.

JOHNNY (CONT'D)
(to Ben)
Come on big guy, you can do it!

INT. SPACE STATION COMMAND CENTER – DAY

Victor watches the shields slide down. Alone. An island.

AUTOMATED VOICE
Event threshold in thirty seconds.

INT. SPACE STATION - CORRIDOR - SAME TIME

Sue races down the hall. Not panicked. With determination.

EXT. SPACE STATION AIR LOCK – DAY

The exterior air lock door slides open. In agonizing, weightless slow motion Ben reaches to haul himself inside.

The leading edge of the cloud hits: Ben is pelted by a hissing mass of space dust, splattering his suit with orange stains. Larger particles, small pellets, pepper him. Ben hauls himself in the last few feet by pulling on his tether.

INT. SPACE STATION AIR LOCK/COMMAND CENTER - DAY

AUTOMATED VOICE
Event threshold in ten seconds. TEN...

Johnny punches controls to close the exterior airlock door...

Reed opens a first aid kit, grabs a thermo-elastic blanket...

INT. SPACE STATION - COMMAND CENTER/OBSERVATION DECK – SAME

Clutching the diamond ring, Victor stands defiantly. Showing absolutely no concern for the others. Interested only in the event itself. Lights and equipment FALL, CRASHING around him.

A control panel EXPLODES in Victor's face. He jumps back, and into the falling equipment. Collapses under the weight.

INT. SPACE STATION - AIR LOCK - SAME TIME

Sue rounds a corner, sees Reed and Johnny.

SUE
Johnny! Reed!

AUTOMATED VOICE
FIVE...FOOOOUUUR...

SLOW MOTION: Everyone frozen in position as:

- JOHNNY is hit with sparks of flame from a control panel.
- REED REACHES out for Ben and the airlock door.
- VAPOR STREAM pours down on Sue from a blown gasket.
- THE SPACE DUST burns into Ben's skin.

SLOW MOTION: Just BEFORE the exterior air-lock door closes, a SINGLE PARTICLE zips through the narrowing gap and hits Ben in the back, ripping through his suit. The exterior door shuts and seals. The station loses all power. DARKNESS.

EXT. SPACE STATION – DAY

As quickly as it came, the cloud passes on and whirls away, leaving the space station intact. Power quietly flickers on.

Silence. Time resumes. All four pick up exactly where they left off, unaware of anything that just happened to them.

INT. SPACE STATION COMMAND CENTER – DAY

Victor emerges from the rubble. He stands, checks his body. A few scrapes, nothing serious. A thin, throbbing CUT on his head. He touches the wound, but it is not bleeding.

INT. SPACE STATION AIR LOCK – DAY

Reed and Johnny scramble to open the interior air lock door. Sue joins them, as they pull Ben in. They try to remove his helmet. We don't see his face, but he's clearly unconscious.

REED
He's not responsive –

JOHNNY
Ben! Ben!

INT. VON DOOM COMPOUND HOSPITAL ROOM - DAY

A BLACK SCREEN:

JOHNNY'S VOICE
Ben, wake up! Wake up!

SUBJECTIVE CAMERA, BEN'S POV: The blurry image of Johnny comes slowly into focus, standing beside a hospital bed.

BEN (O.S.)
Where...where am I?

JOHNNY
Back on Earth. Victor's medical facility... We're in quarantine.

BEN (O.S.)
Reed?... Sue?

JOHNNY
They're fine. Everybody *else*...is fine.

Johnny looks away, as if he can't bear to lay eyes on him.

BEN (O.S.)
What's wrong with me?

JOHNNY
I swear to you they've done everything humanly possible. The best plastic surgeons in the world, Ben. You had the best—

BEN (O.S.)
Give me a mirror...

Johnny picks up a hand mirror on the bed table before Ben can reach it, reluctant to give it to him.

JOHNNY
They said that's not such a good idea, the shock alone could—

BEN (O.S.)
Give me the god damn mirror!

Ben grabs it from him. Then slowly raises it to look and see that...except for some serious stubble, Ben's totally normal.

JOHNNY
Unfortunately, the doctors just couldn't do anything to fix your face!

He cackles as he heads for the door. Ben heaves the mirror at him, breaking it into hundreds of pieces. He turns to the side-table, and grabs that picture of DEBBIE. It calms him.

EXT. VON DOOM COMPOUND - ESTABLISHING – DAY

A modern facility of glass and stone, nestled in the forest. In stark contrast to the lush greenery surrounding it.

INT. VON DOOM COMPOUND HOSPITAL CORRIDOR/SUE'S ROOM – DAY

Reed walks down the hall. His hair is GRAYING at the temples. He passes Johnny, who is smiling, still enjoying his joke on Ben. Johnny slows, looking at Reed's hair.

JOHNNY
Nice 'do. Going for the "grandpa" look?

Reed passes a mirror, slowing, seeing his gray hairs. He keeps going. He passes a partially open door. He stops when he catches a glimpse of Sue asleep in bed. He sees a vase of flowers in the hall. He grabs a couple lilies, and enters.

But Reed sees...the room is already FILLED with expensive flowers. All from VICTOR. Reed is trumped once again.

A DOCTOR writes on Sue's chart. A wall TV

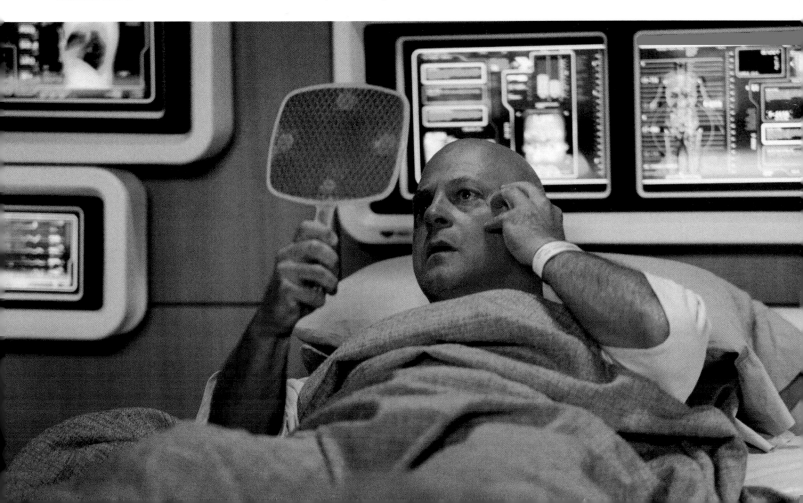

plays a press conference with Victor, outside the FACILITY. He looks worse for wear. A few hairs out of place, and a small BANDAGE on his face. We PUSH INTO the press conference—

REPORTER #1
You've been accused in the past of moving science a little too fast—

VICTOR
Accused by who? My competitors?

REPORTER #2
But surely this accident gives you pause—

VICTOR
Danger is <u>always</u> part of discovery. What would have happened if Ben Franklin never went out in a storm? Without risk, there's no reward.

REPORTER #3
So where's the reward? You promised a cure-all.

Victor pauses. For the first time. Just a flicker.

VICTOR
And you'll have it. I've never come up short. And I'm not going to start now.

REPORTER #2
So you're still taking VDI public—

VICTOR
Yes, of course. I've never been more confident in the compan—

Reed mutes the television.

REED
How's she doing?

DOCTOR
Stable. Vitals are strong.

Reed takes the clipboard, looks for himself.

REED
Blood panels show no irradiation. Good. You'll step up this protocol, every—

DOCTOR
Four hours. We know what we're doing... One more day of observation, then you're all cleared.

The Doctor takes his clipboard, and walks out. Reed steps to Sue, with the drooping flowers in hand. Quiet:

REED
Sue...I want to tell you...I'm...

WHOOSH. A NURSE rolls in with a tray bearing ten more extravagant bouquets. Reed looks resigned. He walks out.

REED (CONT'D)
She's allergic to orchids. Put that *Amaryllis Apapathos* by her bed. The African lilies? They're her favorites.

Reed exits, dropping his two wilted lilies into the trash.

Sue opens one eye, as the big lilies land by the bed.

INT. VON DOOM COMPOUND HOSPITAL ROOM – DAY

A SEXY NURSE wheels a testing station into Johnny's room. He's stripped down to Calvins, changing into a ski outfit.

SEXY NURSE
And where do we think we're going?

JOHNNY
I don't know if "we've" noticed, but the sickest runs this side of the Alps are *right outside that window*—

NURSE
I've noticed... But doctor's orders, you're not allowed to leave until we—

JOHNNY
Finish the tests, I know - could you give me a hand with this zipper?

NURSE
You know this is not a ski resort.

JOHNNY
Not <u>yet</u>.

Johnny opens the cardboard box, revealing a colorful fiberglass object the size of a briefcase. In the blink of an eye, he unfolds it into a LONG SNOWBOARD.

JOHNNY (CONT'D)
Luckily grandma still sends care packages.

The nurse pops a thermometer in his mouth to shut him up.

NURSE
You are trouble.

JOHNNY
(thermometer in his mouth)
Brubbles my Triddle Name.

They both pay more attention to his zipper than the digital read-out: it runs right up past 98.6, then accelerates fast.

SEXY NURSE
You're hot!

JOHNNY
So are you!

SEXY NURSE
I mean, you feel a little feverish.

JOHNNY
I've never felt better in my life. When do you get off work?

SEXY NURSE
My shift ends at four, but I couldn't—

JOHNNY
Meet me at 4:01, top of the run. That'll give you a minute to freshen up.

He hands her the thermometer, a quick kiss and he's out the door. The machine beeps: Johnny's temperature is 209 DEGREES.

EXT. VON DOOM COMPOUND HOSPITAL PATIO - DAY

Ben finds Reed on a patio with a panoramic view. Reed works at a laptop computer.

BEN
How long was I out?

REED
Three days. I was worried about you. How are you feeling?

BEN
Solid.

Ben can see Reed doesn't look too solid.

BEN (CONT'D)
How you doing?

Reed shakes his head, looking back at his screen.

REED
I don't know. I just keep going over and over the numbers.

BEN
Reed. Even you can't compute every little thing.

REED
I should have done more, run more tests—

Ben gets closer, pushing down Reed's computer screen.

BEN
It was a freak of nature. Last I checked, you don't have a crystal ball. Let it go.

Reed considers. But he can't let it go. He opens his computer back up, returning to work. Ben shakes his head, looks out at the view. His eyes catch on something, wheels turning.

BEN (CONT'D)
You go through something like this, makes you appreciate having the right woman in your life.

REED
Yeah, you and Debbie are perfect—

BEN
Reed, I'm not talking about Debbie.

Reed follows Ben's eyes to a lower level patio: SUE.

REED
What? Come on. She's got a good thing with Victor—

BEN
I'm sorry, did that cosmic-bath loosen your screws?

REED
He's smart, powerful, successful—

BEN
Well maybe you should date him.

Reed looks at Ben, resigned.

REED
Ben. He'll give her the life she deserves. She ended up with the right guy. Things worked out for the best.

Reed steps away. Ben stands alone, an idea sparking.

BEN
Do I have to do everything myself?

INT. HELICOPTER/EXT. MOUNTAIN SUMMIT – DAY

The chopper hovers over this pristine peak. JOHNNY and his NURSE sit in the chopper-bay, prepping their ski-gear. Johnny's customized snowboard has wild, acrylic patterns.

His Nurse wears a hot pink cat-suit, her skis dangling out. Their bodies are close; a sexy, competitive flirtation. They look down at a death-defying black diamond run.

JOHNNY
Me like-y.

SEXY NURSE
Stay right. Left is trouble.

JOHNNY
I thought we went over this.

SEXY NURSE
Last one down springs for room service.

She pulls down her goggles, jumps out. Johnny drops after her, hitting the snow. He smolders: literally. The snow bank behind him sizzles and starts to melt.

He takes off after her and the chase is on:

EXT. BLACK DIAMOND RUN – DAY

The Nurse knows every inch of the trail, slicing expertly in and out of the trees through deep powder. Johnny's a speed freak, maximizing velocity, closing the gap between them.

Ghostly FLAMES shoot off his hair: his ski cap catches fire, flies off. Jets of fire knife through the back of his jacket.

The Nurse looks back: In a burst of speed, Johnny draws even. She looks over and sees the flames shooting out behind him...

SEXY NURSE
You're on fire!

JOHNNY
Not this again—

SEXY NURSE
No: You're ON FIRE!

Johnny sees his gloves are burning, flicks them off in alarm. His body SHUDDERS: the back of his ski suit catches on fire. A burst of flame launches him down the slope like a rocket.

Nurse loses concentration, falls. Johnny races away like a missile, screaming in exhilaration. He looks back - no nurse.

He tries to put out his flaming clothes, and accidentally VEERS to the LEFT. He fails to notice the giant CHASM in front of him. He faces forward and...

SCREEAAMMS! LAUNCHING off the cliff, LEGS FLAILING, trying to catch ground. FLAMES begin to TRAIL his body as he FALLS towards the rocks below. He tries to will his body away.

Instead, his body becomes engulfed in flame. He is a HUMAN TORCH! And for a moment he HOLDS THE AIR — the fire giving him some kind of...LIFT. He maneuvers just over the rocks, almost making a 90 degree turn.

He looks back at the rocks in disbelief. But the lift doesn't last long. He quickly CRASHES, landing HARD into a snowbank.

He opens his eyes; tries to move but can't. He's trapped under snow and ice. With all his strength, he tries to move, NO DICE. Panic sets in. His eyes go wide as the snow around quickly begins to melt. Johnny is on fire, and within seconds he's sitting in a small POND, steam rising from the water.

The nurse races toward the steam. Scared,

panicked. She finds Johnny...smiling, sitting naked in an impromptu hot tub, staring at his hands. His body. Exhilarated.

JOHNNY
Care to join me?

She smiles and unzips. The FLAMES DISSOLVE TO...CANDLES IN—

EXT. VON DOOM COMPOUND VICTOR'S OFFICE – DAY

On an expansive parapet with a billion-dollar view, Victor prepares a romantic dinner-setting as his staff scurry about. He checks every fork and knife, with a slightly manic energy.

VICTOR
How's the IPO?

LEONARD
Stable. We're looking at low twenties. It's a good number, considering the fallout from—

VICTOR
Reed's disaster. You know, I half-think he did this to me on purpose.

LEONARD
Sir, I'm sure he wouldn't put himself—

But Victor is on to the next thought, always strategizing.

VICTOR
Get me on the AM shows, Larry King, cover of the Journal...
(staring into silver tray)
I've got to do something about this scar. Make sure they only shoot my right side.

LEONARD
Actually, uh, people seem to think the scar "humanizes" you.

VICTOR
And that's a good thing?

Victor looks at the scar, enraged by this defect. It glistens in the silver tray. His eyes are bloodshot, sleepless.

LEONARD
You know, maybe you should get some rest—

VICTOR
Later. First, I've got some unfinished business. A deal that needs closing...

Leonard looks at the table, the lavish spread. A beat.

LEONARD
Sir. I've always wondered... Why Sue? You could have any woman in the world but—

VICTOR
That's why. Because I could have any other woman... You know, when they asked Caesar "why England," he said, "because it's not mine."

INT. VON DOOM COMPOUND DINING

HALL - LATE AFTERNOON

Two dozen EMPLOYEES sit and eat. Others serve themselves at the buffet. Ben and Sue walk into the dining hall—

SUE
I can only stay for one drink, Ben, I've got to meet with Victor.

BEN
Wouldn't want to keep Vic waiting.

They turn a corner and find Reed, entering by another door.

BEN (CONT'D)
Hey Reed, what are you doing here?
(before he can answer)
Great, why don't you join us?

He quickly shepherds the two of them toward a quiet table. Ben's stomach GROWLS; so loud that they all can hear it.

BEN (CONT'D)
God, I'm starving. Gonna hit the buffet.

Ben's stomach growls again, even louder this time.

INT. VON DOOM COMPOUND DINING HALL – EVENING

The sun is long gone, and so are most of the diners. The room is darker, more romantic. Ben finishes the last shrimp on his plate, pushes it away, belches prodigiously.

BEN
Pardon me...

Sue and Reed stare at him. Ben's stomach growls *again*.

REED
Are you alright?

BEN
I think I need to lie down. Bad shrimp.

This was Ben's plan, but he *really* isn't feeling well, unsteady when he walks away. He looks down at his stomach.

BEN (CONT'D)
Really bad shrimp.

ANGLE: Fireplace. Sue looks gorgeous in the light. A beat. A long beat. Reed doesn't know where to start with this woman.

REED
Feeling better?

SUE
Yes, thanks.

REED
That's good. That's uh...good.

SUE
You always had a way with words.
(an awkward beat)

I should be getting back.

Sue gets up to leave. Exasperated, Reed tries to think of something, anything, to say.

REED
I'm really happy for you and Victor.

She slows down, looking at him. She was hoping for more.

SUE
You're <u>happy</u> for me and Victor.

REED
I can tell you guys are enjoying what was the best part of our relationship—

SUE
Which was?

REED
Passion.

We see surprise on Sue's face, and...

REED (CONT'D)
For science.

SUE
(frustrated)
You are such a dork, Reed... You never got it and never will unless it's explained to you in quantum physics.

As if triggered by her emotion, the fireplace light around her BENDS. The flames flicker in a ghostly breeze.

REED
What? What did I say?

She looks more disappointed than angry.

SUE
It's never what you say. It's what you don't say. What you don't do...

She lets that hang. A lot of history here. Quiet, hurt - she wants Reed to fight for her, to show some emotion.

REED
I...I...I just wanted to—

As Sue's emotions swirl, she slowly...*disappears*.

SUE
It's been two years, and all you can say is you're <u>happy</u> for me and some other guy...
(standing up, hurt)
You know, Victor may be a lot of things, but at least he's not afraid to fight for what he wants...
(Reed looks down)
And it's nice to be wanted sometimes. To be heard...seen... Reed, look at me.

He looks up...but all that's left of her is the blush on her cheek and her bewitching eyes. He drops his fork, shocked.

REED
Uh, Sue..? I <u>can't</u>.

SUE
What? What do you mean you—

REED
Sue...*look at your hands*.

She raises her hands, but we don't see them. We only see a medical wristband...floating. Her watch...floating. Her clothes appear to be suspended in mid air.

<u>Sue is invisible</u>. She shrieks and gets up — knocking a GLASS off the table...

SLOW MOTION: The glass flies off the table, tumbling... Reed instinctively reaches for the bottle: his arm stretches two feet out of his sleeve — grabs it just before it hits—

Then snaps back into place. Reed stares at his arm in disbelief. Sue's eyes widen as well. The rest of Sue reappears. They look at each other: mutual alarm.

JOHNNY (O.S.)
You guys will not believe what just happened!

They look up to see JOHNNY in the doorway, NAKED except for the nurse's PINK PARKA wrapped around his midsection.

INT. VON DOOM COMPOUND - VICTOR'S OFFICE - EARLY EVENING

CLUNK. The candles burn low on the table. Victor strides out, heading for the door. He runs his hand through his hair to comb some strays. A CLUMP comes off in his fingers. He PAUSES. He steps to a mirror, stares at his hair. His <u>SCAR</u>.

It is longer than the bandage now (as if it SPREAD). Victor peels back the bandage, and sees the scar is bluish-gray. Deep, unhealthy, maybe infected...

INT. VON DOOM COMPOUND - HALL-WAY - EARLY EVENING

DOUBLE DOORS burst open. Reed, Sue, and Johnny urgently walk.

SUE
It has to be the cloud. It's fundamentally altered our DNA.

REED
Let's not jump to conclusions, we need a *massive amount of evidence* before making that leap.

Reed's glances over his shoulder. He stares. Sue follows his gaze to see: Johnny's FINGERTIPS are on fire. He SNAPS his fingers. They GO OUT. He's totally unharmed.

JOHNNY
Now what is up with *that?*

REED
(deadpan)
The cloud has fundamentally altered our DNA.

JOHNNY
Cool. What'd it do to you guys?

SUE
Apparently I can disappear.

JOHNNY
Please tell me you go silent too.

Only one thing on Reed's mind—

REED
We have to find Ben.

EXT. VON DOOM COMPOUND - OUT-SIDE BEN'S ROOM - EARLY EVENING

Johnny snaps his fingers — which generate small explosive bursts of flame. He turns it on and off, like the "CLAPPER."

JOHNNY
Flame on, flame off. Flame on, flame off—

SUE
Johnny.

He does it again. Flame on, flame off.

SUE (CONT'D)
Stop it.

JOHNNY
Okay, "mom."

Reed's about to knock on Ben's door when he hears the banging, moaning and pleading inside. Johnny smiles.

JOHNNY (CONT'D)
Oh, you dawg you. Better not be my nurse!

INT. VON DOOM COMPOUND - BEN'S ROOM - EARLY EVENING

REED (O.S.)
Ben, are you there?

A creepy rippling movement begins beneath the sheet and gradually intensifies, reflected in the fabric's surface: the contours of Ben's body are changing, inflating, growing rough and craggy. SOUND of grinding heavy rocks.

SUE (O.S.)
Open up Ben, we need to talk.

It all stops. A beat, then all four legs of the bed give way and it crashes to the floor. Under the covers, he groans in pain, and his voice is DEEPER, GRAVELY, but definitely CLEAR:

BEN
LEAVE ME ALONE!!!

INT. VON DOOM COMPOUND - OUTSIDE BEN'S ROOM - EARLY EVENING

Reed decides they can't wait any longer. He kneels to the floor. He concentrates, not sure if it will work... Suddenly, his arm STRETCHES, THIN ENOUGH TO CREEP UNDER THE DOORJAMB.

INT. VON DOOM COMPOUND - BEN'S ROOM - EARLY EVENING

Reed's arm wriggles under the door. It bends upward, swiping clumsily, until it finally grabs the knob. Rubbery fingers find the latch and unlock the door.

INT. VON DOOM COMPOUND - OUTSIDE BEN'S ROOM - EARLY EVENING

Reed focuses, and pulls. His arm snakes out from under the door and snaps back into place. His flesh and bones reforming before their eyes. Johnny stares at Reed.

JOHNNY
Ewwwwwwww. That is disgusting.

They hear a tremendous SMASH from inside the room.

INT. VON DOOM COMPOUND - BEN'S ROOM - EARLY EVENING

They open the door. The room is trashed. Every stick of furniture smashed to splinters.

REED
...Ben?

Their eyes adjust; there's a huge hole where the window used to be. They rush to it. Looking out they see SOMETHING LARGE in the distance, running away.

JOHNNY
What is that *thing?*

SUE
I think that thing is Ben.

Reed looks out, emotions roiling. Is that his best friend..? Suddenly, Victor comes around the corner (bandage bigger).

VICTOR
What's going on?

SUE
Victor, are you feeling alright?

He considers, but never shows weakness. He nods.

VICTOR
Just a little banged up. A couple scrapes. Why?

REED
Ben did this.

VICTOR
Ben did this?

REED
He's had some kind of...reaction to exposure from the cloud. And he's not the only one.

SUE
We need to find him.

Victor redirects his attention to Sue.

SUE (CONT'D)
Victor, I'm sorry I—

VICTOR
(cold)
Just find him.

Victor strides off, leaving the others.

JOHNNY
Anybody know where the big guy's going?

We PUSH IN on a picture of Debbie lying on the floor, Reed knows exactly where Ben is going.

REED
He's going home.

EXT. TRAIN YARD - NIGHT

A view from Brooklyn: Manhattan glistens in the distance. CAMERA MOVES down to A TRAIN YARD, where we find empty cargo trains. We PUSH IN on the main track, where...

A CARGO TRAIN has just stopped. We hear a cargo DOOR slide open, then WHUMP! Big FEET hit the ground. Someone, or someTHING barrels into the night.

EXT. BIG & TALL SHOP - NIGHT

A locked storefront on Flatbush Ave. SOUND of breaking glass.

INT. BIG & TALL SHOP - NIGHT

SERIES OF SHOTS: Ben tries on clothes, shoes. Jackets rip, shoes split. He needs an extra extra extra large.

EXT. PAY PHONE - NIGHT

A HUGE FIGURE is huddled in shadow. It's Ben.

CLOSE ON: The dial pad. Big fingers try to push keys but they're too large. Ben tries for a few seconds, getting more and more frustrated. He manages to press "0" with his pinky.

BEN
Hello, Operator?

Ben looks up the street, into the 2nd story window of a modest, working-class home. His eyes go soft when he sees Debbie grab the phone.

BEN (CONT'D)
Deb... It's me. I need you to step out front.

DEBBIE
Out front? You home, baby? I got a surprise for you.

He blinks hard. Sad, dark.

BEN
I got a surprise for you too.

EXT. BROOKLYN HOUSE - NIGHT

Debbie steps out. There is "WELCOME HOME" sign over the door. She looks out. The wind blows softly. Something shifts in the darkness. Debbie pulls her robe tighter.

DEBBIE
Ben?

BEN (O.S.)
Don't come any closer for a sec. This is gonna be kind of a shock... You remember when we said "together forever no matter what"?

DEBBIE
Baby, you're scaring me.

A hanging beat. And Ben...steps into the light, where we SEE HIM FOR THE FIRST TIME: he's HUGE, easily twice the size he once was, and AN ORANGY ROCKY SURFACE COVERS HIS ENTIRE BODY.

Debbie sees him. Fear washes over her, not sure what to think. He reaches out, a little tentative. She flinches back.

DEBBIE (CONT'D)
Oh my G-g-g. What did you...do to Ben?

BEN
Deb, it's me. It's still me.

He reaches out. She recoils. It's too much for her. Tears swell in her eyes. Covering her mouth, she backs away.

He takes a step closer. She backs away faster, tripping over her robe, falling into the street. A car screeches to a halt. Ben instinctively steps out to help, but she scurries back.

DEBBIE
Don't...don't...DON'T TOUCH ME!

Her shout wakes NEIGHBORS. Lights flicker on. Ben knows he has to go. He looks at Debbie, sensing this is the last time he'll see her. She trembles, terrified. His eyes go moist.

BEN
I love you, Deb.

With that, he turns away. The "WELCOME HOME" sign flutters, falls to the ground. A tragic tableau. As more lights go on around him, Ben picks up his pace, speeding into the dawn.

INT. VICTOR'S COMPOUND OFFICE - DAY

Victor packs a monogrammed Armani briefcase: "VDM" emblazoned on a gold plate. Leonard waits not-so-patiently.

VICTOR
Make sure you find Ben, bring him back here. And keep it quiet. I don't need this to hit the press.

LEONARD
Yes sir. You've got the Mayor at eight, then a nine-thirty interview with the Journal—

VICTOR
Front page?

LEONARD
Top left, like you asked.
(a smile)
Today Wall Street. Tomorrow, who knows...maybe Washington.

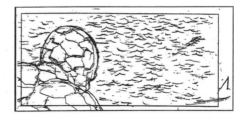

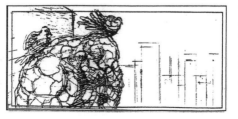
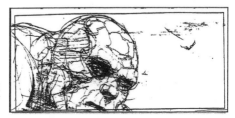

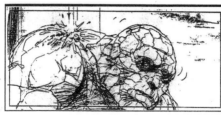

Victor turns to Leonard, disappointed with him.

VICTOR
Leonard. Think bigger.

EXT. BROOKLYN BRIDGE - DAY

We swoop toward this epic monument. On a steel girder above the road, we see...a STATUE. <u>BEN</u>. He sits on the edge of the beams, staring down at the river below, brooding, muttering.

BEN
A few days in space, it'll be great, what's the worst that could happen?

A PIGEON flutters past him, and drops a white gooey gift on his shoulder. Ben just glares up at the heavens.

BEN (CONT'D)
Perfect. Thanks.

He hears the sound of someone SOBBING. He turns to see...a distraught BUSINESSMAN with a briefcase. The man drops his case, which PLUMMETS hundreds-of-feet into the RIVER.

The Businessman looks out, ready to jump. He doesn't see Ben (or doesn't realize Ben is not a statue).

BEN (CONT'D)
You think you got trouble? Take a good look, pal, how bad could it be?

The Businessman look at Ben, terrified. Ben steps forward.

BEN (CONT'D)
Okay, easy there, buddy.

Backpedaling, the man SLIPS, <u>FALLING</u> toward the ROADWAY! His arms flail, grabbing a narrow beam — his fingers hold tight while his legs thrash over speeding traffic. Cars and trucks SKIM right underfoot. Ben shakes his head.

BEN (CONT'D)
You <u>had</u> to choose my spot, didn't you?

Ben steps out to help, but...his WEIGHT BENDS the beam! The Businessman LOSES HIS GRIP! He FALLS TO THE ROAD, landing hard on the highway! A few PEDESTRIANS see Ben. They point.

Ben looks up, deer in headlights. He sees a massive TRUCK bearing down on the Businessman.

BEN (CONT'D)
This is <u>really</u> not my day.

Ben DROPS to the street. WHOOMPF! He lands in front of the Businessman, SWEEPS him out of the way with one arm, and turns to the oncoming 18 WHEELER CAB.

The DRIVER slams his brakes, eyes wide. The truck SWERVES, but cannot stop! Time slows to syrup, as Ben looks a little <u>scared</u>. He shuts his eyes, and...

SHOULDER-BLOCKS the INCOMING TRUCK! A football move. The truck BUCKLES, POPPING a WHEELIE, CRUMPLING all the way to the windshield! It looks like a metal car-compactor.

The truck SWERVES hard, its tail SMASHING into steel girders. CARS SCREECH, SWERVE, SLAMMING INTO EACH OTHER, CAUSING A <u>FOUR-LANE TRAFFIC ACCIDENT!</u> Windows shatter, fires flicker. One of the cars is an NYPD CRUISER. COPS clamber out.

EXT. CAB ON HIGHWAY - DAY

Reed, Johnny, and Sue sit in the back. They see the action on the bridge. Reed and Sue lock eyes, sensing the worst.

EXT. BROOKLYN BRIDGE - DAY

Ben stands in the middle of the chaos, staring at the destruction. He sees the tow-truck DRIVER bleeding, trapped in his cab. Ben moves to this burning hunk of steel.

He SWIPES through the shattered window, and PUNCHES the airbag, POPPING it like a kid's balloon. He tries to grab the seat-belt, but his fingers are TOO BIG. He struggles.

BEN
A little help here?! You wanna hit that button, sir?

The driver is too woozy. Ben can't get to the button. Frustrated, he simply TEARS OFF THE DOOR, and RIPS THE DRIVER'S SEAT right out of the cab! COPS round the corner. They see Ben holding onto the Driver. They raise their guns.

COP
FREEZE! PUT THE MAN <u>AND</u> THE SEAT DOWN!

Ben looks at the cops. PEDESTRIANS stare, point. He realizes how he must look - a monster holding a bloody man in hand.

EXT. BROOKLYN BRIDGE - APPROACH - DAY

At the back of the traffic jam, cars SCREECH to stops. The whole bridge is FULL of bumper-to-bumper traffic. We PUSH TOWARD one car: three doors pop open, and out come...

REED, JOHNNY, SUE. They look through smoke and mayhem to see...their first full look at Ben. Reed stands gutpunched.

JOHNNY
Not even Ben deserves that.

EXT. BROOKLYN BRIDGE - DAY

Ben puts the seat down, with the Driver on it. He lunges behind a truck. The cops try to follow, but FLAMES push them back. Ben lurches away, head down, self-conscious.

He tries to hide from ONLOOKERS around him and PEDESTRIANS on walkways overhead. He wants to escape, but he hears SCREAMING MOTORISTS. He grits his teeth, and moves to help them.

EXT. BROOKLYN BRIDGE - GRIDLOCK - DAY

Reed, Sue, and Johnny race toward the flames. All other people head in the OPPOSITE DIRECTION. BRIDGE POLICE herd the crowd away from the accident.

BRIDGE COP
Back! We're evac-ing the bridge.

Reed, Sue, and Johnny slow down, swap glances.

SUE
What now? Reed..? What do we do?

MOVE IN ON REED. A first test of leadership. But he is <u>not</u> a leader. Not yet. Sue gets closer to him.

SUE (CONT'D)
Ben's out there. Let's go get him.

BRIDGE COP
Maybe you didn't hear me. Those cars are gonna blow sky high, any second.

REED
Look, we've got a friend out there in trouble. We need to get to him before—

BRIDGE COP#2
Nobody gets past this point.

A hard beat. Reed signals Sue with a look, a nod.

SUE
What?

REED
(mutters)
We need to get past them.

He motions to her body. She understands. She concentrates, and starts to turn invisible.

BRIDGE COP#1
What the hell is this? A magic show?

But her clothes don't go invisible. Beat. Reed mutters:

REED
Sue. Your clothes. Lose them.

SUE
What..?
(realizes)
<u>Oh.</u>

She unbuttons her blouse. Not thrilled with the idea. She wriggles out of her pants. Down to her skivvies. She reaches back to undo her bra...momentarily loses concentration and becomes visible. The sight of Sue in her undies grabs the COPS attention. Everyone watches, stunned.

The realization that she is visible hits her like a ton of bricks. Cops are transfixed. So is Reed.

JOHNNY
This is so wrong in so many ways.

REED
You've been working out.

SUE
Shut up.

Sue takes a deep breath. Closes her eyes. Focuses. Nothing happens. She's embarrassed and furious.

SUE (CONT'D)
Any more ideas, Reed? Maybe <u>you</u> should strip

down next, see how it feels to have fifty people staring—

...and she DISAPPEARS. Entirely. Undies float. Jaws drop.

REED
Uh, Sue?

She stops ranting. Realizes she's gone invisible.

SUE (INVISIBLE)
Oh. Well then...

The undies drop. The cops stare open-mouthed. They turn to look at Reed, astonished. He sheepishly shrugs his shoulders.

JOHNNY
I'm gonna need serious therapy.

A beat. She walks away. The cops watch her, gaping. By the time they turn back around, Reed and Johnny are gone, disappearing into the clouds of smoke.

EXT. BROOKLYN BRIDGE - DAY

A news CHOPPER flies around the bridge, fighting for the best angle on the action.

EXT. BROOKLYN BRIDGE - ACCIDENT - DAY

Reed races through wreckage. He tries to see over a big TRUCK, and his neck STREEETCHES!

He finally sees...<u>BEN</u>. Reed wraps around a car, and...BOO! His face snakes right in front of Ben. Ben jumps.

BEN
What the—!

REED
Ben. Are you okay?

BEN
Am I okay?! You wanna explain that?!

He motions to Reed's neck. Then to his own body:

BEN (CONT'D)
Or this?! What the hell am I? 'Cause I sure ain't Ben anymore.

Reed opens his mouth, but he has no answer. Not yet.

SUE (O.S.)
REED! BEN! LOOK OUT!

Ben spins, looking for Sue. He can't see her. But he does see...A CAR INCHES AWAY, WITH GAS TANK FLAMING!

BOOOOM! The first car BLOWS! BOOOM!BOOOOM!BOOOOOM! Empty cars BLOW in a chain-reaction. The flames are mushrooming!

Reed SWIPES his ARMS OUT, holding people back. His arms FLATTEN to form a barricade — FACES INDENT his skin.

FLAMES lash out. A pack of attractive YOUNG WOMEN scream. Johnny LEAPS toward them. His feet LEAVE THE GROUND, giving him extra lift. He SPINS, lands, and embraces the women, SHIELDING them from flames which burn up his back. He looks the ladies up and down, and gives a cheesy smile.

Sue SCREAMS. She puts her hands up (a normal reflex). The air seems to RIPPLE around her hands, like FORCE-FIELDS.

She looks at them, surprised, confused. Her invisible fields SPIRAL OUT, partially <u>CONTAINING</u> the blast. But the flames hurtle closer. She fights the pressure. Blood trickles from her nose. Just as the white hot blast is about to hit her...

Sue is dressed again. Visible. She SCREAMS, and PUSHES THE FORCE DOWN INTO THE ROAD! She collapses, as the blast deflects off the street and into...

An oncoming FIRETRUCK! BOOOOM! The firetruck is KNOCKED OFF THE GROUND, SLEWING SIDEWAYS. Brakes scream. Its tail slashes out, PUNCHING though the guard-rail.

THE BACK OF THE TRUCK DANGLES OUT, HUNDREDS OF FEET ABOVE THE WATER! FIREMEN hang off the back and sides. The truck TEETERS, falling! Ben wastes no time. He GRABS onto the front of the truck, just as it goes off the side!

He DIGS his heels into the ground, but his feet

DRAG across the concrete, digging grooves into the street.

ON THE DANGLING FIRETRUCK: FIREMEN climb out, clawing toward the bridge. Their truck SWINGS. Bits and pieces tumble down at them - a hose, an axe, a helmet. All deadly now. The HANGING LADDER swoops down, with men RIDING ON IT!

Ben SCREAMS! STRAINING with all his might. Ben SCREAMS! His muscles ripple, and...he takes his first step...back. Another scream. Another step. Another. Another. Epic, painful.

He is pulling the truck back onto the bridge, inch by inch. His footsteps THUD. With monumental effort, he levels the truck. Firemen scurry over hoses and ladders, some climbing over Ben.

Reed tends to Sue who has fainted from her effort. Ben steps back from the truck and slumps to the street exhausted. Wary cops close in to cover him with weapons, but...

The FIREMEN slowly begin to APPLAUD. The crowd of onlookers joins in as well. Sue, Reed, and Johnny seem surprised, touched by the reaction. But Ben seems uncomfortable.

Fireman step forward to offer Reed a couple of their coats; he hands one to Johnny and uses the other to cover Sue.

EXT. BROOKLYN BRIDGE - DAY

Ben sees a familiar face in the masses: DEBBIE. Ben steps toward her, but she stops him with a look. She places something on the ground and runs off into the crowd.

Ben sees something GLISTENING on the ground. He stoops over to pick up...her ENGAGEMENT RING. His big fingers can't grip it. He tries in vain. Hopeless, pathetic. A beat. And...

A hand grabs the ring. It's Reed. Quiet, close.

REED
I swear to you, I will do everything in my power until there is not a breath left in me: you are going to be Ben again.

Off the wounded look in Ben's eyes, wanting to believe him...

INT. VICTOR'S OFFICE DAY - DAY

Victor sits with remote in hand, staring at his plasma TV. ON THE TV: he sees a crowd of firemen applauding the new Fantastic Four. For the first time they strike a heroic pose. Leonard enters, with a phone in his hand.

LEONARD
Uh, sir...Larry King called, to cancel.
(seeing the TV, a beat)
Apparently, there's a bigger story.

Victor sees Reed put his arms around Sue as he covers her with the jacket. And the penny

drops: he's FURIOUS. As it hits him, he feels something odd. He looks down at his hand...at glints of gleaming METAL poking through flesh.

EXT/INT. EMERGENCY HOLDING AREA - DAY

An impromptu command center — a series of police tents, surrounded by EMERGENCY VEHICLES, NEWS VANS, FIRETRUCKS.

INT. EMERGENCY HOLDING AREA - TENT - DAY

Reed, Sue, Ben and Johnny sit together, getting changed. They get ready to go, but the CHIEF FIREMAN enters, stopping them.

CHIEF FIREMAN
There's some folks outside, want to talk to you.

REED
We're not going public with this. We're scientists, not celebrities.

CHIEF FIREMAN
Too late, son.

He turns on a little TV MONITOR in the corner. NEWS FOOTAGE plays on all stations, with the tagline: FANTASTIC FOUR.

CHIEF FIREMAN (CONT'D)
That's what they're calling you. The Fantastic Four.

JOHNNY
Nice.

Johnny heads for the exit.

SUE
Johnny, slow down. Let's think this through, a second.

Johnny pauses. Rubs his chin once. And...

JOHNNY
Okay. Done thinking.

He runs out. Sue, Ben, and Reed swap glances, knowing Johnny cannot be their spokesman. They take off after him, out to—

EXT. EMERGENCY HOLDING AREA - PRESS FIELD - DAY

CLICKCLICKCLICK! Fifty cameras flash. The field is full of press. Our heroes freeze, shocked by the crowd.

Johnny eats up the attention. Ben turns, self-conscious. Reed notices. The Chief Fireman turns to them.

CHIEF FIREMAN
So which one of you's the leader?

Johnny does not hesitate.

JOHNNY
That'd be me.

The film brings the not-yet-so-Fantastic Four together to try out their new powers during a huge action sequence that was filmed on a partial scale set of New York's Brooklyn Bridge. When The Thing climbs the bridge in a moment of despair, he actually encounters a jumper and tries to save him, but all hell breaks loose. Soon Sue, Reed and Johnny arrive on the scene. As crazy as it looks on film, director Tim Story says it was worse behind the scenes. "It was the hardest thing in the world!" he laments. "The real Brooklyn Bridge in New York City is maybe a mile long, and we only built 300 feet of it. To do the amount of action we did in one section of the bridge, we really needed 800 feet."

Detailing how they blocked out the massive sequence, Story explains, "Within the 300 feet we had many different sets, and any time I wanted something moved, it would take between five and six hours to move to the next set and be ready to shoot. We would have to do everything in a day, and then they would move it all overnight. The next time we showed up it would be a different set, whether it was the fire truck, or the crash scene, or just the traffic going through. It was always a time problem because if I didn't finish my day, and let's say I wanted to come back and only use a quarter of the day to get another scene, I couldn't do it. If I did that, the rest of the day would be gone, because of the hours it took to move the set. The weather in Vancouver was also a factor. We were shooting at the start of winter and it would rain on us. Unlike Los Angeles rain, when it rains in Vancouver, it rains for a week. It doesn't stop or let

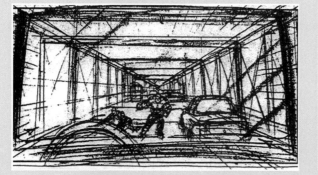

This spread: One of the movie's most memorable moments, The Thing vs. a large truck, was storyboarded carefully to ensure maximum impact onscreen.

up! We had big tents over our heads to block out the rain. It was just one of those sequences that was so difficult to do.

"We had to constantly move around and mind you, it's a big accident scene, so there were no places to move equipment," he continues. "We had to climb over cars to get to certain scenes. It was one of the hardest things we've ever done. We would do the shoots in small increments, four days here and three days there. We came back to the set about three times, not to mention the second unit stuff that was being done — they were back about four times. We had a number of days there and the factors of shooting on the set were just complicated by the weather, the extras and the fact we had explosions. There was fire all over the place, and wires to pull Johnny, because he does a flying thing on the bridge. Then you can't forget we had Michael Chiklis in his Thing suit. It was really tough to be in that, and we always had to be conscious of how long he was in it, because it just drained him of all his

energy. We probably threw every complication we could actually throw at ourselves in that sequence. We even had children and animals!"

Another particular challenge was that the sequence featured a huge amount of visual effects work. "It had so many effects," Story says. "We had a blue screen towering above us, all the way around in 360 degrees. Every shot in the sequence is an effects shot, no matter what! The special effects stuff we had to shoot took forever and a day. But Kurt Williams, our visual effects supervisor, came up with some of the greatest shots."

"We wanted to get the effect of being in a helicopter flying right along the bridge, to get a shot of the car crash," executive producer Ralph Winter adds. "So we set up a camera car with a crane on it next to the bridge set — we could drive at the same speed as the car crash, and get one take of that high-speed action, while we're moving and they're moving. We had to figure out logistically how to make that work and make it safe."

One element of the bridge sequence finds The

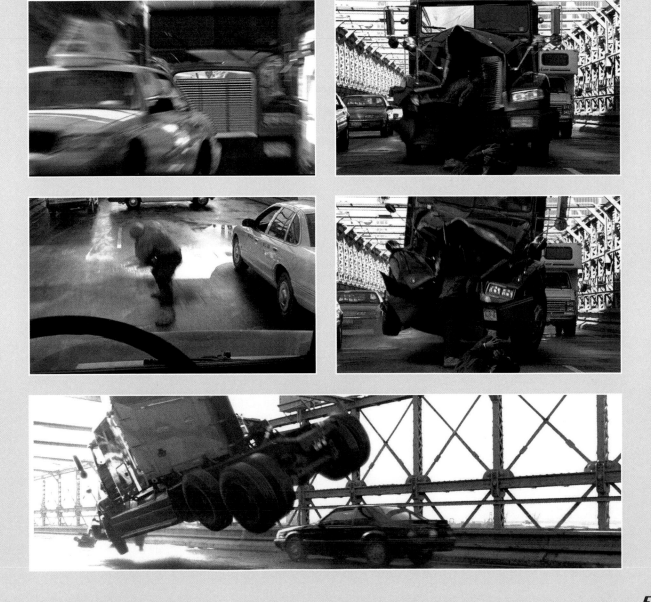

This spread: The Thing drags a fire truck to safety. It might look like the Brooklyn Bridge, but the whole scene was shot in a parking lot in Vancouver.

Thing bodily stopping an eighteen-wheel truck. "We storyboarded it before we built the bridge," Winter says. "We actually sunk a 40,000-pound cement weight, and then set up steel anchors on top of that, bolted to the weight that the truck would crash into, to simulate the impact of hitting The Thing. It's a bit of experimentation and trial and error with the crushing of the truck to get it to work just the way you want." (It was worth the effort: the final shot was so effective, it was given pride of place in the film's first teaser trailer.)

A fire truck also goes over the side of the bridge, Winter relates: "To get some of the shots, we were on a separate parking lot away from the bridge set, with a very large crane holding a fire truck seventy-five feet up in the air. Then we put our actors on it, and the camera below it. When we came back the next day, we rigged it differently and got ourselves up on the top of the fire truck at seventy-five feet in the air, looking down. We spread the blue screen on the asphalt, which allowed us to separate the truck from the 'water' below, which was added later in post-production."

"At the end of the day, we had this 300-foot part of the Brooklyn Bridge and when you see the finished shots, you actually believe they are on *the* Brooklyn Bridge," Tim Story concludes. "It brings a whole other level to what you are doing. When you see Brooklyn in the background and you start to *believe* where you are, that's when things take a twist and you get pumped up. I have to admit, I'm extremely happy about the scene."

CHIEF FIREMAN
No seriously.

A beat. Sue and Ben turn to Reed. The Chief hands him a mic.

CHIEF FIREMAN (CONT'D)
You're on, son. They'll want a statement.

All eyes go to Reed. He looks out, gulps hard. A long beat.

REED
Uh, during our recent mission to the Von Doom space station, we were exposed to as yet-unidentified radioactive energy, most probably some kind of nucleotide compoun—

Nobody came for a science class. A crush of questions overwhelms Reed:

VARIOUS REPORTERS
What happened on the bridge? Does it hurt to stretch? Were you really on fire? Is it true that one of you can fly?

JOHNNY
Working on it. And it's a lot harder—

SUE
We don't know much more than you do, at this point. Which is why we will be going directly to the lab, where we can diagnose our symptoms and—

REPORTER #2
Symptoms? So this is a disease?

Reed looks at Ben's face, feeling the guilt. Ben is lost in thought, looking at Deb's ENGAGE-MENT RING. Johnny leaps in.

JOHNNY
Symptoms? Please. If having powers is a disease, then yeah we got it. And we are gonna blow your minds. There's a new day dawning. The day of the Fantastic Four.

REPORTER #3
That thing doesn't look too fantastic.

The Reporter nods toward Ben. Ben's fists tighten, the sound of rocks crushing together. Reed feels his pain.

REED
Ben Grimm is a genuine American hero who's been through a terrible orde—

JOHNNY
What he's trying to say is: every team needs a mascot...

Reporters laugh. Ben turns his head away. Reed burns.

REED
Look, we went up to space to find a way to understand DNA, to cure disease, save lives. Well, now it's our DNA, our disease, our lives on the line...
(a beat)
Thank you. No more questions.

Reed, Sue, and Ben get up to go. The press waits a beat, then surges. Ben spins, holding up one finger. A giant.

BEN
Be nice.

The press step back, intimidated. Flashbulbs POP, and Ben's FACE FREEZES. It goes BLACK-AND-WHITE on a NEW YORK POST in—

EXT. BANK - DAY

Establishing shot of a historic New York building.

INT. BANK - CONFERENCE ROOM - CONTINUOUS

BANKERS sit around a table. LAPTOPS hum. The lead banker is power-broker NED CECIL. The men keep their eyes on Victor.

NED CECIL
Well, Victor, the bank would like to congratulate you. On the fastest freefall since the Depression. We can't even give your stock away.

VICTOR
Ned, you know I can turn this around.

Ned motions to the paper, the picture of BEN.

NED CECIL
You promised a cure-all, and came back with this. Who the hell's going to invest in a biotech company that turns its workers into circus freaks?

Victor's grip tightens around the table, and...the LAPTOPS FLICKER, losing feeds.

Victor looks down at his hands - a private beat (did I do that?) He lets go of the table; screens go back to normal.

VICTOR
(pointed)
I really appreciate all your support.

NED CECIL
You've got a week, Victor. One week to turn this around. Or we pull out....
(a beat)
This meeting is over.

Victor looks at him, blood boiling, and we CUT HARD TO—

INT. BANK - HALLWAY - DAY

Victor and Leonard stride out. Victor is writhing.

VICTOR
Goddamn book-keeper doesn't know preferred stock from livestock.

Leonard is thinking all business.

LEONARD
Sir. Reed's comments at that press conference killed us. How are we going to turn this

around?

Victor considers. His mind races, eyes narrow.

VICTOR
Very simple. I cure them. If I can cure these freaks, then I can cure anyone. What better way to restore my reputation?

Leonard nods, impressed. Victor is a man in motion. As they step into sunlight, we cut to...CLICKCLICKCLICK in—

EXT. BAXTER BUILDING - DAY

REPORTERS snap pictures. A POLICE CONVOY drives up, stopping in front of a towering HIGH-RISE. Sue, Reed, and Johnny get out of a police-car. Ben steps out of a BIG PADDY-WAGON, which immediately bounces back up to the normal axle position.

COPS hold back the surging press. Ben keeps his head down, self-conscious. He passes Johnny, smiling for the cameras.

JOHNNY
Smile, Ben. They want to like you. Give 'em your good side. Or your less bad side.

Ben turns to a group of LITTLE KIDS. Stiff, tentative:

BEN
Uh...don't do drugs.

The kids FLINCH. Ben trudges on. Johnny smiles bright, doing hand-signs for F4. Sue pulls him toward—

INT. BAXTER BUILDING - LOBBY - DAY

The Fantastic Four enter. They are greeted by JIMMY O'HOOLIHAN, an old-time doorman with a kind smile.

O'HOOLIHAN
Welcome back to the Baxter, Dr. Richards. All that for you?

He motions to the flashing cameras outside.

REED
I'm afraid so...

He searches for the name. Sue steps up.

SUE
Jimmy. Good to see you again.

He smiles at Sue, then at Reed.

O'HOOLIHAN
Good to see you too... Don't worry, sir. I know how crowded that head of yours is.

REED
Any visitors while I was away?

O'HOOLIHAN
Just the usual. Told 'em you were circling round outer space.

He opens a drawer full of LETTERS from the

BANK. Reed looks sheepish. He shuts the drawer, looks to Johnny and Sue.

REED
We had a tough year.

BEN
Yeah, nine years straight.

Reed looks at Ben. Thanks a lot. DING. Elevator doors open.

INT. BAXTER BUILDING - ELEVATOR - DAY

They enter. Reed hits the top button, for the 20TH FLOOR.

JOHNNY
Twenty? From outside the place looks a lot taller.

REED
Oh, it is.

The doors close, but...the ELEVATOR does not move. A beat.

JOHNNY
Either we're moving really fast...or not at all.

A digital readout on the panel: EXCEED MAXIMUM WEIGHT. A sign reads: MAXIMUM CAPACITY: 2000 pounds. They turn to Ben.

BEN
I'll take the stairs.

SOUND BITES

Ioan Gruffudd
"Stan Lee! What a character. He is *wonderful*. He came down to play a postman for the day, a tiny little cameo in the movie. And he injected such a fabulous energy and the spirit of how we tried to make this movie. He was so full of life. He was amazing."

Doors open. He lumbers out. As the doors close behind him, he looks back over his shoulder, locking eyes with Reed.

INT. BAXTER BUILDING - ELEVATOR - DAY

The elevator rises. Reed roils with guilt.

SUE
How come Ben can't turn it on and off like us?

REED
That's what we're here to find out.

SUE
If it happened to him, then it could...

Happen to all of them. Reed nods softly.

JOHNNY
Wait. You mean there's a chance we could be full-on-24-7-fantastic?

SUE
Grow up, Johnny. You want to run around <u>on fire</u> for the rest of your life?

JOHNNY
Is that a trick question? C'mon, I can't be the only one who thinks this is cool.

Reed considers. But Sue cuts him short with a look.

DING! The elevator stops.

INT. BAXTER BUILDING - ATRIUM - MOMENTS LATER

The elevator opens. They step out. They might be on the 20th floor, but Reed owns the building from here to floor sixty. It's a massive atrium, lit by skylights far above—

Reed leads them into another area filled with separate "apartments" and all the amenities of home.

REED
We should stay here until we can define the extent of our changes...

JOHNNY
This place is deluxe. You got cable?

REED
(hearing Ben's FOOTSTEPS)
...and figure out how to reverse them. Let me show you to your rooms.

THE BAXTER BUILDING

"The vision I had for the Baxter Building was that it was the lair of an absent-minded professor, and that was the concept we used for the design," says production designer Bill Boes, who teamed up with set decorator Elizabeth Wilcox to bring the Fantastic Four's fabled headquarters to life. "The building is like a thirty-floor monument to Reed Richards' experiments, a real hi-tech scientific junkyard, a hodgepodge of half-finished creations and experiments. You can see how Reed has built this place from the ground up, one piece on top of the other. When he gets a grant, or comes into some money, he builds another piece and it just keeps going and going."

Contrasting the dark mausoleum that is Boes' design for Victor Von Doom's building, he conceptualized the Baxter Building as a tangled mess of beauty. "We started with how the building was created. Reed bought the building when he was in school, and just kept adding on to it from there. It's originally an art-deco building: on the exterior, there's a lot of brick, with a creamy art-deco look. But there's also rosettes, new

Right: Some of the exteriors were shot at the Art Deco Marine Building in Vancouver.

Opposite: Is that the Fantasticar on the Baxter Building's landing pad?

aluminum, and lots of cylinders and vertical pieces."

"Tim Story told me that he wanted a 'New York daytime' look for the film, kind of serene with lots of color, especially with the look of the Baxter Building," Boes continues. "We were able to find newspaper boxes, tree guards, New York hot dog stands, silver fire hydrants — all of which give the film a strong New York feel, especially in regards to the exterior of the building. We also went to New York to film some plate shots." Boes was also careful to reference Jack Kirby's original design: "I modeled the look of the Baxter Building entirely from the comic books. I actually wanted a cross-section of the different looks over the years." There are some intriguing details to look out for: "On the roof, which sort of looks like a helicopter pad, we put this half-finished vehicle, which appears in the film but is rather ambiguous, because we want fans to speculate as to what it might be. Is it the Fantasticar? It might be!

"The one consistent look to the exterior and interior of the Baxter Building is the use of Art Deco," says Boes. (Indeed, some exteriors, and the scenes set in the building's lobby were shot at a famous Art Deco landmark, the Marine Building in Vancouver.) "For the interior, we wanted an amalgamation of Reed's inven-

Opposite and below: Reed Richards' lab, from production designs to the final set.

tions, lots of different ideas, but with the top floor, the living area, being a nice 'family' space," Boes continues. "Reed's office is really a penthouse and his inventions are everywhere. There's part of a Sputnik near his work area! There's a main lab with a large rotunda and there's also a plant lab, for mutation experiments, and a hydroponics area, all very organic-looking. For the look of the interiors, there's lots of tile, mixed with wood. The floor of Reed's main lab used to be the exterior roof of another building, for example.

Boes wanted the interior of the Baxter Building to be a mixture of both contemporary technology and retro looks. "It's very eclectic: there's a lamp from the 1930s, but the building is filled with 1950s-style horizontal arches, and the bedrooms have a 1960s retro look to them, especially Sue's bedroom," he says. "My goal was to be faithful to the comic books; we haven't left anything out. There's an observation room where the team tests out their powers. There's a computer lab, a workshop with drills and tools, and an observatory on top of the building that comes directly from the comic books. The living area has a pool table and a television with a dish, and it feels like a real home away from the rest of the building. You believe that a normal family could live here."

LIVING/KITCHEN 3.00

Opposite and above: The Baxter Building's comfortable 'family' living quarters, from design to realisation.

Left: A concept design for Reed's office.

EXT. BAXTER BUILDING - DAY

The press has died down, but there are still plenty of cameras. A MAYBACH SEDAN rolls up. Victor emerges, wearing sunglasses. This time, the press pay no attention to him. No cameras flash. Victor tightens, and enters the building.

INT. SUE'S ROOM - DAY

Sue walks out of the bathroom in a robe, drying her hair. She notices a familiar book on a shelf: a SCRAPBOOK.

She flips through it. It's filled with pictures of Reed and his inventions — a lot less fancy than Victor's multimedia globe. She stops at a picture of her and Reed in COLLEGE.

A noise, and she turns, flinching slightly, surprised to see...VICTOR. He smiles, standing at the door, watching her.

VICTOR
God, I've been so worried about you.

She notices the scar on his head.

SUE
Victor, your scar—

VICTOR
I told you, I'm fine. It's you I'm worried about.

SUE
I'm sorry I didn't get a chance to—

VICTOR
Please, no apologies. I've arranged for your things to be moved to one of my condos. You'll have round-the-clock care.

He goes for her bag. But she stops him. A half beat.

SUE
Thank you, that's generous, but I think I should stay here. With my brother. Until we get a handle on this.

Victor is not used to being rebuffed. He gives a thin smile.

VICTOR
Sue. I think you should let my doctors have a look at you.

A tense beat. Standoff. Made more tense by—

REED (O.S.)
Victor! What are you doing here?

They turn to see Reed approaching, with files in hand.

VICTOR
I'm starting to wonder the same thing... How much do you know about what happened to you?

REED
Not much. We need to run tests to see the extent of the damage.

Victor pauses. He looks at Sue, knowing she's here to stay.

VICTOR
Well, let me know if there is anything I can do. We're all in this together now.

Victor shakes Reed's hand. His GRIP is so tight that Reed's fingers STRETCH. Victor lets go, and turns to Sue, who puts her hand out. He smiles, and shakes. He heads off.

Reed looks at his hand. Shakes his wrist. He looks at Victor.

INT. BAXTER BUILDING - HALL - DAY

Victor moves fast, holds tight to his anger. Reed catches up.

REED
Victor, wait... I just wanted to say, I'm sorry the mission didn't go as planned—

Victor suddenly WHEELS on Reed. Lights flicker.

VICTOR
Didn't go as planned? It was a catastrophe. You ruined the lives of four people—

REED
I ruined? With all due respect, I told you to abort—

VICTOR
Abort? Reed, I put my company, my name, billions of dollars on the line, and I will not let you make me look like a fool—

REED
Victor, if we could understand what happened to us—

VICTOR
I don't want to understand it. This isn't one of your science projects. I just want to fix it. Fast!

Reed sees Victor's SCAR maybe growing. Lights dim.

VOICE (O.S.)
There a problem, Vic?

They turn to see...BEN down the hall, leaning in a doorway. Victor tightens, looking at Ben's massive rock-hewn body.

VICTOR
No problem, Ben.

He turns back to Reed. Close, quiet. Lights flicker.

VICTOR (CONT'D)
Just pay your goddamn electric bill, and get to work on a cure.

Victor steps away, toward the elevator. He passes Ben, who just smiles and waves "goodbye." Before Victor's finger taps the down-button, the button lights up (as if the circuit responded to him). Reed exhales, shaken. Victor steps into—

INT. BAXTER BUILDING - ELEVATOR - DAY

The doors close, and Victor really LETS LOOSE. He SLAMS his fist into a STEEL WALL. The wall BUCKLES, steel DENTING.

Victor shakes out his hand, and sees...a rippling METALLIC SHELL under the skin. He stares at it in horror. The dark surface pulsates with electric energy. What is he becoming..?

INT. BAXTER BUILDING LABS - DAY

Sue works the controls. Reed approaches Ben with an ELECTRODE NEEDLE. He tries to stick the needle into Ben, but it SNAPS.

BEN
You got a chisel round here?

REED
If we're going to identify the source of the mutation, we need to isolate your recombinant DNA so we can activate positional genomes.

Ben looks to Sue for translation.

SUE
We need to give you a physical, so we know what got zapped.

BEN
Well why didn't you say so? You want me to lift some weights or something?

Reed shakes his head. He approaches with an X-RAY MACHINE.

REED
No, just sit back. We have a good sense of your strength from the firetruck. We need to find the source of your strength.

He turns on the X-ray machine. The graph shows SOLID ROCK. The rays don't penetrate. Sue and Reed look confused.

BEN
How bad is it? You know I used to smoke.

Reed grabs a BLOOD PRESSURE MACHINE, but the strap is way too short to wrap around Ben's arm. Reed stands stumped. He looks at his tray full of instruments. He picks up the little rubber REFLEX-HAMMER. But it looks miniscule compared to Ben.

Reed has an idea. He opens a drawer full of HARDWARE TOOLS. He pulls out a real HAMMER. He approaches Ben.

REED
Okay, this might smart a little.

He taps Ben's knee lightly, and BEN'S LEG KICKS! SLAMMING UP! RIGHT BETWEEN REED'S LEGS! The ultimate kick in the crotch. Reed STRETCHES UP a few feet, then SNAPS BACK, wincing.

REED (CONT'D)
(high-pitched voice)

We'll...continue this later.

INT. BAXTER BUILDING LABS - DAY

From their second level control room, Reed and Sue observe Johnny in an enclosed fire-proof chamber. Flames escape through the vents of the chamber... he's fully torched!

Reed watches the read-out: it climbs from 2000 to 4000 degrees Kelvin. They are essentially taking his temperature.

INSIDE THE CHAMBER: Johnny turns white hot, blinding to look at: the chamber walls begin to glow red. Machines go haywire.

His feet even start to LIFT OFF THE GROUND, LEVITATING a foot or two. He looks down, excited, burning hotter and hotter.

REED
Back it down, Johnny!

JOHNNY
I can go hotter!

He won't stop. Reed pulls a switch on the wall. FOAM sprays out of nozzles, dousing Johnny's flames. He stands there, covered in thick FOAM. His body steams. So does his temper.

JOHNNY (CONT'D)
You're really cramping my style here.

SUE
You were at 4000 Kelvin. Any hotter, you're approaching supernova—

JOHNNY
Sweet.

SUE
That's the temperature of the <u>sun</u>.

REED
Not only could you kill yourself, but you could set fire to Earth's atmosphere and destroy all human life as we know it.

JOHNNY
Gotcha. Okay. Supernova bad.

Reed looks at the control panels.

SUE
He cooked the equipment.

Frustrated, Reed looks at the smoking system. And we CUT TO—

INT. BAXTER BUILDING - LAB - DAY

Reed and Ben sit in chairs, facing each other. A beat passes. Ben taps his fingers on the chair, making small DENTS. Reed looks down at his clipboard. A little awkward.

REED
Okay. I've uh, got some questions, from Sue. That she thought might be better coming from me... Can you, you know, go to the bathroom...like normal...

BEN
Yeah.
(a beat)
You don't wanna know the details.

REED
Ben, I'm afraid I've got to ask—

BEN
Not unless you want that clipboard stretched up your—

REED
O-kay. We'll skip that question.

INT. BAXTER BUILDING - LAB - DAY

Reed and Johnny now. Johnny exercises. Reed stands nearby. Clipboard in hand.

REED
Is there something about flames? About flaming, that you—

JOHNNY
What are you trying to say? Just because I dress well and like to dance—

REED
(confused)
What? No. I'm trying to figure out why we each ended up with different symptoms.

JOHNNY
Oh, well that's easy: I'm hot. You're...well, you're a little limp. Sue's easy to see through. And Ben's always been a hardass.
(a beat)
Why aren't you writing this down?

Reed sighs. It's going to be a long process.

INT. BAXTER BUILDING LAB - DAY

Reed and Sue, tables turned: Reed observes her through a prismatic device measuring light refraction. He "sees" her through the device: lit up like some heavenly creature. He's having a hard time concentrating. He focuses on his work.

REED
It's not "invisibility" per se. You're bending the light around you with some kind of malleable force field. That's what you projected on the Bridge.

SUE
What about you? You haven't eaten in days. How come you're never on this side of the microscope?

He tightens, uncomfortable with being center of attention. She reaches for his arm, like a specimen. He pulls away, but she sees a glimpse of BRUISES on his ARMS. She slows down.

SUE (CONT'D)
Bruises...from the bridge?

He nods, rolls down his sleeves.

REED
Have you had any side-effects, from your powers?

She considers. A little vulnerable.

SUE
I've had some headaches. Migraines.

A beat. Reed drops his eyes, makes a note, back to work.

REED
You should be able to bend light around other objects, even people, if you could control your emotional state better—

SUE
Excuse me?

She is annoyed. Reed is oblivious.

REED
I'm saying, if you had a little more self control, you could locate the trigger. Can you remember your exact emotions when—

SUE
Anger. Rage. Frustration.

REED
Okay. Is there any way to duplicate that feeling? Some memory or...

SUE
(staring right at him)
I'm sure I can come up with something.

She looks at Reed, eyes narrow. She becomes invisible. As she focuses on Reed - and gets angry - a small, clear FORCE-FIELD forms around her body. The force-field BENDS LIGHT around a MICROSCOPE, which goes INVISIBLE. Reed steps out to ask...

REED
How's that coming — whoa—

The FORCE-FIELD shoots in all directions, knocking everything over in a fifteen foot radius. Reed is thrown from his chair.

SUE
I'm sorry, I'm sorry, I didn't mean to do that... You must think that was some kind of latent hostility or—

REED
What in the world would give me that idea?

An awkward beat.

REED (CONT'D)
I mean, you broke up with me, right?

SUE
Are you kidding?

REED
No, I distinctly remember: you walked out my door. Ergo...

She didn't want to get into this. She looks down, vulnerable.

SUE
Reed. I was ready for the next step, you weren't, ergo, I walked.

REED
I think it was a little more complicated than—

SUE
I just wanted to share an apartment. What was so complicated about that?

The question stumps him. A beat. He struggles.

REED
There were a lot of variables to consider—

SUE
No. There weren't. There was you. And me. No variables, no math. It was actually the simplest thing in the world. But your head got in the way...like it always does.

Her words penetrate. He knows she's right. He looks away.

REED
Sue...I just...I thought...

He struggles for the words.

SUE
Same old Reed. Too much thinking...

He opens his mouth, but...WHAM! Doors open. Johnny enters, wearing a CHARRED SHIRT. He points to the burned scraps of his shirt.

JOHNNY
Okay guys, we have a serious problem.

INT. BAXTER BUILDING LABS - DAY

ANGLES of Reed in the lab, grabbing their space uniforms from various closets/containers:

REED (V.O.)
Our uniforms were exposed to the storm like us. So they can transform like us, becoming invisible, changing size on demand or remaining impervious to flame.

REVEAL: Reed, Sue, and Johnny step out to look at themselves in a mirror wearing the uniforms. No boots, no gloves. Not yet. (The uniforms will develop, like our heroes).

BEN
You look like an eighties rock band.

SUE
(to Ben)
The suit will stretch. You should try it—

BEN
I wouldn't be caught dead in that.

JOHNNY
He's right. These costumes are...missing something. I can't put my finger on it—

REED
They're not costumes.

SUE
We're not taking them out. Johnny, we need to stay here till we've stabilized.

Johnny shakes his head, frustrated.

JOHNNY
I'm getting sick of being trapped here. NASA wasn't even this strict!

He marches out. Sue turns to Reed, who says nothing. Sue heads out, leaving Ben and Reed. A beat. Ben looks at Reed.

BEN
(looking at uniform)
Maybe it's missing a utility belt.

Off Reed's dark look, we hear:

VICTOR (V.O.)
So what's the prognosis?

INT. VON DOOM INDUSTRIES - VICTOR'S OFFICE - DAY

CLOSE ON: an X-RAY. Victor's ARM. The metallic transformation is higher now. PULL BACK TO REVEAL: Victor and his DOCTOR. In the wall behind them: ancient armor (maybe we noticed it before, maybe not). It adds a little menace to the room.

DOCTOR
Your tissue, your organs, your entire biophysical structure is changing. Every system is still functioning, somehow—

VICTOR
And they're changing into...

DOCTOR
I don't really know. A compound organicmetallic alloy. Stronger than titanium or carbon steel. Harder than diamonds—

VICTOR
Like the shields Reed said would protect us.
(cold fury, deadly focus)
How long?

DOCTOR
At this rate, the infection should be complete in two, maybe three weeks—

VICTOR
What do you mean "complete"?

DOCTOR
I wish I could tell you. I can't pretend to know what we're dealing with here. I'll notify the CDC and—

Victor hardens, razor sharp.

VICTOR
What?

DOCTOR
The Center for Disease Control. If this thing is contagious—

WHHM! Victor GRABS the Doctor by the throat.

VICTOR
Look at me. I have a life. I'm the face of a billion-dollar-company... We need to keep this confidential, understand? Victor's grip TIGHTENS around the man's throat.

DOCTOR
But...this disease...is progressive... degenerative...

VICTOR
That's terrible news...

With one cobra-swift move, Victor thrusts his metallic arm into the doctor, killing him instantly. Victor retracts his arm, and looks at it, shocked by his own strength.

VICTOR (CONT'D)
...but I think I'll get a second opinion.

INT. BAXTER BUILDING - REED'S OFFICE - NIGHT

A SERIES OF TIME-LAPSE SHOTS: REED works around the Baxter Building, spending hours searching for the cure. He checks charts, writes equations, paces, frustrated.

Finally, he sits at his long desk, looking at a wall where Ben's CHARTS are projected (both Ben and Thing's anatomies). Reed wears the uniform under his labcoat. He checks his equations over and over, making notes upon notes.

REED
Nothing...nothing...nothing...

He hits the end of the slides. The wall fills with white light. Frustrated, Reed SLAMS his head into his desk, CRASH! Something FALLS off the end of the desk.

Reed raises his head, revealing his flattened face. He steps over to see...a PLANT SAMPLE from space, glass box shattered. Red sparks swirl around the plant, like the cosmic storm.

REED (CONT'D)
Of course...of course...the cloud...

THE COSMIC STORM swirls, terrifying. We slowly PULL BACK TO—

INT. BAXTER BUILDING - MAIN LAB - NIGHT

The STORM is a computer-image on screen now. Behind the screen are six chalkboards full of Reed's calculations and the scribbled beginnings of a MACHINE.

We PULL BACK to see his arm stretched across the room writing on the end of another chalkboard.

SUITING UP

 or costume designer Jose Fernandez, a life-long *Fantastic Four* fan, getting the chance to conceptualize the look of the comic book characters for the movie was a dream come true. For the Fantastic Four themselves, Fernandez began with one thought: spandex. "I'd used leather on my previous films, so I was looking to try something different," says Fernandez. "Spandex seemed like the perfect fit for the Fantastic Four's costumes."

Fernandez's creations first appear at the start of the film, during the fateful trip into space. "We built flight suits for them, which is what they're wearing in space — but they're also wearing their spandex suits underneath," Fernandez reveals. "We had about ten identical suits for each actor, because they take such a beating in the film. They each took about eight weeks to build. We wanted to make them look structured, and like the suits from the comic books, but not look cheesy — which is what people expect spandex to look like. The biggest challenge was getting the right proportions for the actors, because they all have different body types. We gave them muscle suits to wear underneath the outfits

Above right: Ben Grimm's new friend Alicia Masters has a bohemian look.

Right and opposite: The Fantastic Four's spandex costumes each took eight weeks to make.

because spandex, which is very dense, can make you look a bit skinny! I think they turned out great."

Alicia Masters was an interesting character for Fernandez to outfit, as actress Kerry Washington offers an entirely new vision of the blind sculptress, which gave the designer more creative freedom. "Alicia was wide open in terms of costume," Fernandez confirms. "She's a bohemian artist, and that's the look we went for. There's no one Alicia costume, but rather a consistent funky thrift-store look throughout the film that's really a collision between Miss Match and a total hodgepodge that Alicia pieces together from different places."

Then there's the small matter of creating costumes for two of the most iconic characters in comic book history: Dr. Doom and The Thing. A tricky job for Fernandez was finding a way to costume The Thing while still allowing Ben Grimm, and the personality of actor Michael Chiklis, to shine through. "When I first met with producer Ralph Winter, he told me that they'd been working on a costume for The Thing for ten years, and that it had been the biggest obstacle in terms of making a *Fantastic Four* film," says Fernandez, who designed the foam suit that Chiklis wears throughout the film. "I did a maquette of The Thing and Ralph and the studio really loved it. The look of The Thing is so important because he sets the tone for the whole film, so getting it right was essential. The entire suit is made of foam, and the body and legs were made up of separate pieces, parts of which were controlled mechanically. Poor Michael Chiklis was trapped in the costume and he could never take it off during filming, however much he wanted to!"

In addition to creating the foam suit, Fernandez also designed several pieces of wardrobe for Ben Grimm to

wear in the film, clothes that demonstrate Ben's acceptance of his new identity as The Thing. "One of the themes in the film is that Ben, in particular, has to learn to accept his powers and learn to live in his rock-covered body," says Fernandez. "When The Thing becomes more comfortable with himself, he wears grey slacks, a trenchcoat, retro Nike shoes and a fedora. I also gave him work-boots and, near the end of the film, cargo pants."

So what about the movie's villain? "I designed a maquette of Dr. Doom's head to show to the studio in Los Angeles," says Fernandez. "They were a bit nervous. There was talk of doing Doom's face as make-up, but I knew that wouldn't work, so I did a maquette — and they liked my design."

From there, Fernandez began the task of outfitting Dr. Doom from top to bottom. "I wanted the costume to have gold buttons, first of all, followed by slacks with stripes, working almost exclusively with green and black," says Fernandez, who worked out of an office at Vancouver Film Studios during filming. "The costume has a high waist, and there's two belts and a shirt made of an Indian fabric. Instead of the traditional cape, we designed more of a grey coat for Doom to wear in the film, and the gold buttons are front and center."

From here, the next challenge was to make sure that the costume, and especially the headpiece, would mesh with Julian McMahon's performance. "The original maquette was created with aluminum and gold clay and was sculpted with wire," says Fernandez. "We then did a sculpture specifically for Julian, put the mask on him and it fit very well. We used clay and fiberglass in designing the head and the body, although the main 'metallic' body is a rubber suit that Julian wears. In the film, the costume 'consumes' Victor. For me, the best thing about Doom's costume design was that it fit Julian McMahon *perfectly*, especially with the eyes. When I put on the mask, I looked stupid, but when Julian put on the mask, you could really see the eyes. Doom's eyes are there, and it's really effective."

Above: Early concept art of a trenchcoated Thing with Alicia Masters.

This page: The beautifully crafted Dr. Doom mask.

Opposite: It's all about the eyes... Julian McMahon in full costume.

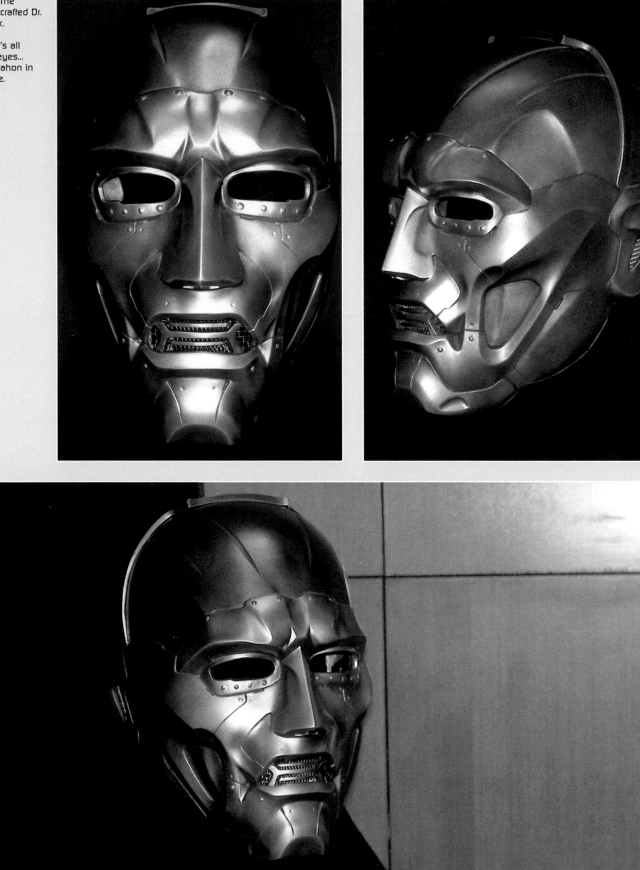

He's moving fast, excited, almost a little manic. He hears...a CREAK. He slows down, but doesn't look up to see Sue enter.

SUE
What are you doing?

REED
(fast, charged)
The plants, from space. Their particles are still charged. With the right amount of energy, those ions could create the elemental profile of the cosmic storm.

He rifles through a desk drawer, then heads out. Sue stands there, looking at the storm. Concerned. Then we CUT TO—

INT. BAXTER BUILDING - HALLWAY - NIGHT

Sue follows Reed. He flips through a file, excited.

REED
If we can build a machine to re-create the storm, we can reverse the polarity—

SUE
(realizing)
And reverse the mutations—

REED
(talking more to himself)
Curing countless diseases, not just ours.

She looks at him.

SUE
But we're the focus, right Reed? Reed..?

REED
Of course. Of course.

SUE
And you sure you can control this thing? Last time didn't work out so well.

REED
(preoccupied, mind spinning)
With the right energy, we can stabilize the storm. Maybe tie into the city grid...

He keeps his head down, making notes, entering—

INT. BAXTER BUILDING - STOREROOM - NIGHT

Reed and Sue enter. Reed is looking for something. Sue slows down, staring at this sprawling space, jam-packed with GEAR, GADGETS, BLUEPRINTS, INVENTIONS. Awe-inspiring, overflowing.

SUE
You really need to get a janitor.

She stares at shelves upon shelves of overcrowded clutter.

SUE (CONT'D)
This must be what it looks like inside your head.

Reed finds his electromicrocope. He turns to Sue, defensive:

REED
There's a system to it.

She starts to pull out a MODEL of the FANTASTICAR.

REED (CONT'D)
Wait! Sue, don't touch tha—

The little car sets the whole shelf off balance. A WAVE OF INVENTIONS COME CLATTERING DOWN! Reed moves fast:

He LUNGES toward Sue, STREEETCHING his ARMS AROUND the SHELF, pushing Sue away, just as the INVENTIONS SMASH TO THE GROUND!

Reed and Sue hit the floor. A close call. Now more closeness: Sue and Reed lay face-to-face, with Reed's arms wrapped around her. A heated beat. Their first real intimate moment.

SUE
Sorry. My fault. I won't...touch anything.

As if suddenly made aware of their vulnerability, Sue and Reed stand, backing off. As they part, we see:

BEN watching from the doorway. Melancholy. He disappears. We slowly MOVE TO...A SURVEILLANCE CAMERA in a VENT GRATE.

INT. VICTOR'S OFFICE - NIGHT

Victor watches a bank of videoscreens. He has the Baxter Building under surveillance. He sees Reed and Sue on monitors. He toys with Sue's diamond ring in his gloved hand.

A door opens. Leonard enters. He sees the screens.

LEONARD
Is Reed any closer to a cure?

Victor looks at that image of Reed and Sue on screen.

VICTOR
The only thing he's closer to is Sue...

But Victor sees something between Reed and Sue on the wall. He leans closer, and the camera ZOOMS IN, as if responding to his will. He ZOOMS all the way to a CLOSE UP of:

REED'S BLUEPRINTS FOR THE TRANSFORMATION CHAMBER. Victor's eyes narrow, mind ticking, a plan forming.

VICTOR (CONT'D)
Make me a reservation for two at Cipriani tonight.

Victor opens a drawer, pulls out an old VIDEOTAPE.

VICTOR (CONT'D)
And get this over to Ben Grimm.

Victor leans forward, fixated on that machine. As he gets closer, his screens go STATICKY. He absentmindedly picks at his SCAR. In shadows, we see skin peeling off.

WOMAN'S VOICE (V.O.)
Close your eyes, baby. Keep 'em closed.

INT. BAXTER BUILDING - MEDIA ROOM - NIGHT

BEN GRIMM stands front and center. Not the Thing. But BEN GRIMM. A normal man. He smiles wide, shaking his head.

WOMAN'S VOICE (V.O.)
You surprised?

Now we PULL BACK to reveal DEBBIE and BEN on a SCREEN. The Thing watches the old videotape. He smiles sadly at his old life. He mouths the words — he knows this tape by heart.

BEN (ON SCREEN)
Yeah I'm surprised. Surprised the fire department didn't shut this down.

ON SCREEN: the handheld camera whips around, revealing...a SURPRISE PARTY. Full of people. Ben Grimm is a popular guy. On screen: Reed hugs Ben. They pose for pictures together.

THE THING
God. I was good looking.

We hear the party sing "HAPPY BIRTHDAY." Debbie kisses Ben. Thing's eyes start to mist. On screen: Ben blows out candles.

DEBBIE (ON SCREEN)
What did you wish for, honey?

BEN (ON SCREEN)
I already got it. Everything I want.

As they kiss, a tear runs down Thing's cheek. The tape ends, and he sits in darkness for a beat. A long, lonely beat.

INT. BAXTER BUILDING - HALLS - NIGHT

Ben stalks the halls, slipping into his ragged trenchcoat. As he passes a crossroads, he sees a strange sight:

REED'S HAND is TIED to a latch in the wall. His ARM is STREEEETCHED THIN, spanning around the corner. Ben just shakes his head, keeps moving. And we FOLLOW REED'S ARM...

UP THE HALL...ROUND A CORNER...DOWN ANOTHER HALL. The muscles and tissue STRETCH, going taut. Finally, we reach...

REED. He steps slowly. He holds a digital TAPE-MEASURE in his other hand, measuring distance. His skin STREEETCHES. His face tightens, pained. We hear the faint SQUEAK of his skin.

VOICE (O.S.)
Damn, Stretch!

Reed turns his head around, seeing JOHNNY come down the hall.

JOHNNY
How far's that rubber bend?

Reed keeps moving, slowly. His muscles and tendons laboring.

REED

That's what I'm trying to calculate. And it's not rubber. It's muscle, tendon. I seem to have the ability to manipulate the malleability of my molecular structure and redistribute my density to—

JOHNNY
Right, whatever, have fun.

And Johnny is GONE, ducking under Reed's arm into—

INT. BAXTER BUILDING - KITCHEN - NIGHT

Johnny opens a cupboard, pulls out some JIFFY POP. It starts to POP in his hand, the bag swelling. He casually turns on a TV, flipping to...the X-GAMES. The Jiffy Pop swells, ready to blow. He rips it open, eats popcorn, and watches the games:

Cool stunts, hot girls. Johnny's brow furrows, a thought forming, a mischievous smile on his lips.

EXT. BAXTER BUILDING - SIDE EXIT - NIGHT

A FIGURE exits, wearing that ragged trench-coat and fedora. Ben disappears into the dark night, and we CUT TO—

EXT. BROOKLYN STREET - NIGHT

Dark. Lights flicker. Steam rises through grates. A shadow emerges. <u>Ben</u>. He heads toward O'DONNEL'S PUB, a classic Brooklyn tavern. Neon sign. Music, life inside. Ben pulls his hat low, turns up his collar, and squeezes through the door into—

INT. O'DONNEL'S PUB - NIGHT

A big photo of Ben Grimm in his astronaut heyday occupies a place over the bar. Ben enters, and the bar goes SILENT. He moves through the crowd. People clear out of the way.

Ben reaches the bar. He sits on a stool, and CRUNCH! SMASH! The stool SNAPS like a toothpick. He hits the ground hard. Glasses shake. A few PATRONS smile, laugh softly.

BEN
That's not funny!

They go silent. They drop bills onto tables, filing out, scared of this monster. ERNIE works

the bar.

ERNIE
Hey, that's Ben Grimm there, the first mook from Brooklyn to go to outer space, so pay him some respect!

But the patrons keep filing out. Ben looks down, weary.

BEN
Ernie. Sorry for killing your business. I'll take the usual, then I'm out... Better make it a double.

Ernie heads for the booze. Ben gives a sad shake of his head. Then he notices...one lone patron at the end of the bar. A beautiful young woman nursing a drink. Meet ALICIA MASTERS.

ALICIA
Who killed the party?

She turns to him, unafraid. He notices her blank stare, lack of focus, and white cane. Alicia is blind.

ERNIE (O.S.)
Made it a triple. On the house, Benny.

Ben takes his drink, but SMASH! His grip shatters the glass, spilling all over himself. He smiles ruefully.

BEN
If there's a God, she hates me.

He grabs a bar-rag to dry off.

ALICIA
I don't think She's real big on hate.

BEN
You wouldn't say that, if you could see me.

She knocks back her drink, grabs her cane, steps toward Ben.

ALICIA
Can I..? See you..?

Ben doesn't say anything. A little unnerved by this woman.

ALICIA (CONT'D)
It's okay, I won't bite...
(feeling his arm)
...not that I could.

She puts a hand on his face - something in her tone and gentle touch allows Ben to let her. She smiles softly.

ALICIA (CONT'D)
Such a sad face... You know, sometimes being different isn't a bad thing.

BEN
Trust me, this ain't one of those times.

She smiles softly, takes her cane, and starts to head out.

ALICIA
See you round, Benny...

Right as she hits the door, over her shoulder—

ALICIA (CONT'D)
I'm Alicia, by the way.

Ben watches her disappear. He sees a few people staring. He lowers his head, turns back to the bar, and finds a new drink, in a steel MAR-TINI SHAKER. He knocks it back.

EXT/INT. UPSCALE RESTAURANT - NIGHT

Lights twinkle. A MAITRE D' leads us through fancy digs. Heads turn, whispers flutter. SUE steps out, joining...Victor at a prime table. He pulls out her chair, wearing gloves.

VICTOR
Thank you for coming out to see me.

She nods, a little self-conscious.

SUE
You said it was urgent.

VICTOR
It is. There's something we need to talk about. Something I need to ask you...

Sue senses where this is going, and she cuts it short.

SUE
(slow, careful)

Victor, wait, slow down a second. I want you to know I appreciate everything you've done for me, but I just don't—

VICTOR
Susan. What are you doing?

He is cold as ice. If he's hurt, he'll never show it.

VICTOR (CONT'D)
You think I brought you here to talk about us? Please. This is business.
(leaning forward, intense)
I need to know: how close is Reed to finding a cure?

She pauses. Then:

SUE
He's working round the clock. But the data needs to be tested, analyzed before—

VICTOR
Same old Reed. All analysis, no action. Wasn't that the problem with you two?

She holds tight, keeping cool.

SUE
If these molecules aren't stable, they could make us worse, maybe even kill us.

VICTOR
Then why is Reed dragging his feet? Maybe he likes having his prize specimen under glass...
(closer, cruel)
It's ironic, isn't it? You're finally the perfect

woman for him...because you're his science project.

The words sting. She can't help but hear some truth in them.

SUE
Please don't make this personal—

VICTOR
Oh, I think you already have.

SUE
Victor, we can't do anything until the research is ready.

Victor's fist CLENCHES — metal SFX.

VICTOR
"We," huh?

Victor SCREECHES his chair back, PUSHING the table so hard that he SPILLS water. Heads turn, all eyes on Sue. Victor gets close to her, too close, a hand on her shoulder.

VICTOR (CONT'D)
Don't forget who you work for, Susan. So get to work. And do your job.

He walks out. As he goes, he slips the engagement ring out of his pocket. He crushes the diamond to dust, leaves the dust in an ashtray, and disappears into the night.

Sue sits embarrassed. She slowly...disappears. People gasp. She walks out, invisible, save for her clothes, which DRIFT through the air. At a TABLE FULL OF BUSINESSMEN—

BUSINESSMAN
I wish my wife would disappear.

The other men laugh, but WHHM! The man's wine SPILLS into his LAP! Sue walks out. The restaurant is left buzzing. Lights twinkle. And we FADE OUT. A beat. Then we CRASH INTO—

EXT. NYC ARENA - ESPN MOTO X GAMES - DAY

The X games in full effect: A maze of mountainous dirt hills and ramps...where MOTO-BIKES launch into the air to the delight of 20,000 fans. The Riders spin and flip, performing aerial acrobatics on their 250CC motor bikes.

X GAMES ANNOUNCER (V.O.)
And now, ladies and gentleman, we have a special guest for you... Johnny Storm of the Fantastic Four!

JOHNNY emerges, wearing his blue uniform, waving to the crowd. He steps up to the pit where RIDERS prep. He beelines to RONNIE RENNER.

JOHNNY
Hey, Ronnie Renner! I'm a big fan.

Ronnie give a tight nod. He doesn't like being upstaged by this circus freak.

The other bikers approach.

KENNY BARTRAM
Heard you like to ride. Wanna take her for a spin?

He motions to his BIKE. Johnny eyes this mean machine.

RONNIE RENNER
Come on, bro. I'll teach you some tricks...if you can keep up.

We PUSH IN on Johnny, his ego getting stoked, as we CUT TO—

INT. NYC ARENA - TRACK - DAY

Ronnie jams down the track, kicking dirt back at Johnny. Johnny now wears a MOTOCROSS OUTFIT over his uniform, with the number "004" on the back and a small 4 over his heart. Ronnie hits the first hill, and CATCHES AIR, FLIPPING HIGH!

X GAMES ANNOUNCER
A rock-solid double-flip!

The CROWD goes wild. Now it's Johnny's turn. He hits the hill, and pulls the exact same move. With even more height!

X GAMES ANNOUNCER (CONT'D)
Look at that lift, ladies and gentlemen!

Johnny sticks the landing. The crowd swells. Ronnie tightens, pulls his throttle harder, taking the next jump, and...MAKING AN INSANE MOVE, CORKSCREWING IN THE AIR!

X GAMES ANNOUNCER (CONT'D)
Frontside 360! He's totally flat and whipped!

He lands clean. The crowd is ready to explode. Johnny REVS his engine, his body starting to STEAM, adrenaline burning. He hits the hill, and pulls an even gnarlier SPIN!

X GAMES ANNOUNCER (CONT'D)
Whoa! That's a...what is that? A 720?

Johnny lands. The crowd roars. Ronnie bears down on the last hill. He leans over his handlebars.

X GAMES ANNOUNCER (CONT'D)
He's going for a Kiss of Death!

Ronnie hits the hill, pulls this JAW-DROPPING DEATH-DEFYING STUNT! The crowd is deafening! Ronnie smiles. And...

JOHNNY SPEEDS FASTER, FASTER. Trails of FLAME start to streak off his back! He RACES LIKE A ROCKET UP THE HILL! LAUNCHING TO IMPOSSIBLE HEIGHTS! SPINNING LIKE A TOP! A FLAMING BLUR!

And now for the really impressive part: Johnny's bike starts to drop, but JOHNNY KEEPS RISING! He FLAMES ON, spiralling upward! For a few seconds, he's actually...almost...flying.

X GAMES ANNOUNCER (CONT'D)
(hand over mic)
Is he......flying?

A beat. Time suspended. And...WHHM! He PLUMMETS back down! LANDS on his bike in mid-air! And sticks a perfect landing, maybe even kicking a little dirt up at Ronnie. Johnny swerves to a stop, with a "holy shit" look on his face. What the hell just happened??

X GAMES ANNOUNCER (CONT'D)
Unbelievable, ladies and gentleman! You've just seen the first...the first...TORCHFLIGHT! The McTORCH!

A new name is born. The crowd goes berserk. Standing ovation. Riders rush up to Johnny. Kenny sees his bike:

The SEAT MELTED, WHEELS BURNED OFF. Johnny smiles.

JOHNNY
My bad. Sorry about that.
(a glance to Ronnie)
Thanks for the lesson, bro.

HOT GIRLS swarm. As Johnny gets swallowed by fans, we see a scary flicker in his eyes: the birth of a star.

INT. BAXTER BUILDING - KITCHEN - MORNING

Sue stands alone, sifting through piles of mail. She focuses on one piece of mail that she's holding. Her hand begins to disappear and then the envelope slowly begins to disappear as well. Sue smiles at the success. Intrigued. Quiet:

SUE
That's new...

Reed enters - overworked, unshaved. He keeps his head down, preoccupied. Sue shifts focus.

SUE (CONT'D)
Have you read these..? From all over. People want us to fight crimes...save their kids...solve their problems...
(no response from Reed)
...when we can't even solve our own.

She puts the letters down, steps closer to Reed.

SUE (CONT'D)
Reed. How close are we to a cure?

REED
No way to know. Without more tests, experiments.

She considers. Victor's words echo in her head.

SUE
We're not specimens, we're patients. This isn't just another science project to you, is it..?

Reed looks up, a little surprised. He opens his mouth, but—

THE X GAMES

Each Fantastic character gets a moment in the film where they experience their powers fully for the first time. Johnny Storm's power moment comes during an X Games sequence. Originally scripted to occur during Johnny's skiing scene, which now has a briefer 'flame on' moment, Tim Story explains they changed venues to better capture the attitude of the most flamboyant member of the Four: "It was a great idea that came from the original script, but we just wanted to make what happens to Johnny at that particular moment in the movie a little more exciting. The X Games is something everybody is into, and Johnny's character is an extreme sports kind of guy. This sequence is an introduction to Johnny's powers and we wanted to create the best stage for that, so that's how the X Games came about."

Story details that the sequence was one of the more hastily produced of the shoot. "We didn't have a lot of time to get this scene together. It almost all came together on a wing and a prayer. Matter of fact, there was no reason why this should have worked out," he laughs. "We were lucky enough to find three of the top six X Games freestyle motorcyclists in the country, and they were available and gung-ho to do the movie. We got a chance to have them as cameos in the film. We also needed a stadium to do it in, and there is a stadium in Vancouver that was available just at the right time, so it worked out perfectly for us. We had all these super sports that these guys were doing. They could already do stupidly amazing stuff on the motorcycles, and then we threw in wirework, having them do double flips that are physically impossible to pull off. It was actually a very fun sequence to do, and one of the few where we had complete control of the environment. We were inside a stadium, so we didn't have to stop shooting for bad weather. That's what you always hope to get, so you can walk away at the end of the day, and then come back the next day and start shooting again. It was one of the few sequences that wasn't hell to do. It was one of the more fun pieces."

Opposite top: Johnny turns up the heat.

Opposite bottom: The enclosed stadium location meant filming was not interrupted by the weather.

Left: Storyboards for jumps achived using wirework, and the first ever Torchflight... the McTorch!

Below: The birth of a star.

BEN (O.S.)
NO...NO... <u>NO FREAKIN' WAY</u>!!

INT. BAXTER BUILDING - MEDIA ROOM - DAY

CRASH! BANG! Ben stalks around the room, furious. Reed and Sue rush in.

REED
BEN! What? What's going on!?

Ben points to the wall-sized TV: the ESPN MOTO X GAMES.

X GAMES REPORTER (ON TV)
So what can you tell us about the outfit?

REVEAL: JOHNNY standing next to an X GAMES REPORTER. He is peeling off the burned remains of his motocross outfit, revealing his FF UNIFORM, with a "4" STITCHED ONTO THE CHEST.

Behind them, STEP UP RIDERS launch their MOTO-BIKES off huge 18' high mountains of dirt, thirty feet in the air.

JOHNNY (ON TV)
Not too much, but I <u>will</u> say it's all weather and no leather. Kind of Armani meets Astronaut.

Ben, Sue, and Reed stare at the wall-sized TV. Mouths agape.

SUE
He didn't.

BEN
Oh, he did.

SUE
<u>What</u> did he do to the uniform?!

She turns to Reed, who gives a sheepish shrug,

and peels back his lapcoat revealing a "4" stitched onto his chest too.

REED
He talked me into it.

X-GAMES REPORTER (ON TV)
So what are your superhero names?

JOHNNY (ON TV)
I go by the Human Torch. The ladies call me Torch.

X-GAMES REPORTER (ON TV)
What about the rest of the team?

Johnny hadn't really thought about them. He spitballs:

JOHNNY (ON TV)
Uh, we call my sister the invisible girl... the Invisible Girl.

SUE
Girl..?!

X-GAMES REPORTER (ON TV)
That's easy to remember. And Reed Richards? He's the leader. So what's he? Mr. Fantastic?

JOHNNY
Well, I wouldn't say he's the leader.

Reed shrugs. He doesn't hate the name.

BEN
Could be worse.

Case in point: a photo of Ben fills the TV.

X-GAMES REPORTER (ON TV)
What about this one? What do you call this Thing?

Johnny smiles, looking right into camera.

JOHNNY
That's it. Just <u>The Thing</u>. We would have gone with The Rock, but it was taken. And "Thing" pretty much sums it up.

A LAUGH from the studio audience.

BEN
(matter-of-fact)
Okay. I'm gonna go kill him now.

He turns to go. Reed wraps an arm around Ben.

REED
Ben! Slow down a second and—

He sees a photo of himself on screen.

X-GAMES REPORTER (ON TV)
Is it true what they say? That he can expand *any* part of his anatomy?

JOHNNY (ON TV)
Actually, between us, I think he's got some problems staying rigid.

REED
(finishing his thought to Ben)
...wait for me...

X-GAMES REPORTER (ON TV)
Which may explain why *this* woman's not smiling.

They put up a shot of Susan.

SUE
I'm driving.

JOHNNY (ON TV)
Dude. That's my sister.

EXT. NYC ARENA - DAY

The Thing rounds the corner. Sees a crowd of girls lined up near a red PORSCHE parked out front...with "TORCHED" on the plates. Ben slows down, smiles.

EXT. NYC ARENA - A LITTLE LATER

Johnny and the Hot Babe exit, signing autographs for girls in the line. Sue and Reed approach, glare like angry parents.

Johnny finds the Valet, who looks ill... his car is gone.

JOHNNY
(looking around)
Where's my ride?

The Valet blows his whistle...and a 4 X 4 solid cube of RED JUNK METAL slides down the street and stops at the curb in front of Johnny. The Valet timidly holds out the keys...

JOHNNY (CONT'D)
What the?! Is that my—

Before he can finish, Johnny gets PELTED IN THE HEAD with the license plate. It rattles to the ground, face up.

Johnny rubs the sting out of his head. Looks up and sees Ben in the distance, dusting off his hands.

JOHNNY (CONT'D)
(shouting: to Ben)
You're gonna pay for that, Pebbles.
(seeing Sue)
What?!

SUE
You gave us <u>names</u>? What are you, the "face" of the Fantastic Four now?

Ben marches up. Hands balled into fists.

BEN
It's about to be a broken face.

REED
This isn't permanent, Johnny. We need to be careful until we're normal again.

JOHNNY
What if some of us don't <u>want</u> to be "normal" again? We didn't <u>all</u> turn into monsters like—

Ben reels back a FIST the size of an anvil. Stops himself. Instead of attacking, he starts to walk off.

Johnny hurls a FIREBALL that SMACKS Ben in the back of the head. Ben stops. Turns around more shocked than hurt.

BEN
Did you just—

Ben gets hit with ANOTHER FIREBALL. This time in the face.

BEN (CONT'D)
Okay that's it, tinkerbell! You want to fly? <u>Fly</u>.

Ben charges like a bull, fist cocked back, and...Reed steps in the way! <u>Too late!</u> WHAMM! Ben's fist PUNCHES INTO REED'S CHEST, which INDENTS. Reed's BACK EXPANDS with Ben's fist, PUNCHING into Johnny, launching Johnny off his feet.

BAM! Johnny SLAMS into a moving ADVERTISING TRUCK, with a BURGER KING flame-broiled WHOPPER on the side. WHOOSH! He leaves a flaming imprint on the all-beef patty.

The crowd stands stunned. So do Reed and Sue. Cameras pop.

Johnny slowly pulls himself up. The paint on the truck begins to bubble around his hand. Beaten, bruised, he stands. Heating up. Both his hands are now <u>flaming fists of fury</u>.

JOHNNY
Let's see if we can get blood from a stone.

He and Ben lock eyes, with a block of sidewalk between them. High Noon. They start to RUN toward each other...

When they are almost within range, Sue STEPS BETWEEN THEM, stops them both in their track with just a look. Like a mom:

SUE
You two need a time-out.

JOHNNY
Blockhead started it!

Ben just stalks off. The crowd clears, scared. A PAPARAZZI snaps a picture. Ben GRABS his camera, and flicks the lens.

EXT. STREETS - DAY

Sue looks at Johnny, more disappointed than angry.

SUE
Damn it, Johnny.

She goes after Ben, leaving Reed and Johnny on the sidewalk.

REED
You need to control yourself and <u>think</u> before you—

JOHNNY
Act. Here we go again. Reed, what if we got these gifts for a <u>reason</u>? What if we have some, you know...like, calling?

REED
A higher calling like getting girls and making money?

Johnny nods, totally missing the sarcasm.

JOHNNY
Is there any higher?

Reed looks at him, disgusted. Johnny waves to the crowd, hand flaming. People SHRIEK, snap pictures. Johnny smiles at Reed.

JOHNNY (CONT'D)
This is who we are, Reed. Accept it. Or better yet: <u>enjoy</u> it.

Johnny steps into the sea of fans. Reed stands alone.

EXT. STREET/ALLEY - DAY

Sue wades through the throng of New Yorkers. Tries to catch up with Ben...whose presence parts the crowd like Moses.

SUE
Ben! Slow down...

Ben glances sideways at her, doesn't stop. She catches up.

SUE (CONT'D)
He didn't mean it. You know Johnny. He's always been a hothead—

BEN
It's not him. It's <u>them</u>.
(pointing to crowd)
I can't live like this.

SUE
Just give Reed a little more time. You know how he works— analyzing every little step before he takes one—

BEN
It's easy for you to be patient.

SUE
No, it's not. I thought I was done waiting for Reed... We're all in this together now, Ben.

He slows down, gets closer, intense.

BEN
Together? Look at me, Susie. You got no idea what I'd give...to be invisible. Your nightmare...is my dream.

She opens her mouth, but has no response. She doesn't know his depth of pain. As he disappears into the alley, we CUT TO—

INT. INVESTMENT BANK - CONFERENCE ROOM - DAY

The news plays on the TV. Head Banker Ned Cecil freezes the screen on an image of...THE THING. He turns to Victor, who sits with the rest of the bankers. Cold, sterile environment.

NED CECIL
This is how you "turn things around"? These freaks are on the front page, and your company's in the obituaries.

Victor has a larger bandage on his face now.

VICTOR
I have a plan to use their publicity for—

NED CECIL
Victor, stop. The bank's lost enough already. This isn't a negotiation. It's a notification. We're pulling out.

A cold, silent beat. Victor leans forward.

VICTOR
You need to look long-term here. Without risk, there's no—

NED CECIL
Reward. We all know the sales pitch, Vic. And frankly, we're done buying... Gentlemen.

He motions to his men. They all stand. Victor is the lone man sitting. PUSH IN on Victor's face, his inner rage palpable. A few quick surges of electricity emanate from his body. This man is getting stronger, more electric.

INT. BANK - UNDERGROUND PARKING STRUCTURE - DAY

After hours. The floor is slick with water - puddles in every direction. Ned Cecil comes out of the elevator, heading for his car. As he goes, the structure lights start to flicker. Ned looks up, watches the lights go out one by one, furthest to closest. He looks around. Unnerved by the darkness.

NED CECIL
Hello..?

A hanging beat. Victor steps out from shadows.

NED CECIL (CONT'D)

(relieved, almost)
Von Doom? Gave me a little shock. No hard feelings, right? Nothing personal.

Victor says nothing. Ned keeps going.

NED CECIL (CONT'D)
You know, you could always move back to Latvura, start fresh.

He mispronounces Latveria, dripping condescension.

NED CECIL (CONT'D)
Maybe that's where you belong, back in the "old country."

That does it. A surge of electricity courses through Victor. His eyes narrow, and the electricity crackles down his leg to THE GROUND. The electric spark hits the water and...

ELECTRIC CURRENTS RACE ACROSS THE GROUND, SLITHERING LIGHTNING-FAST ACROSS THE WATER (like deadly electric snakes), heading straight for Ned. His eyes go wide. And...

NED IS ELECTROCUTED! His body spasms. THUD! He slumps, dead. Smoke rises from his body. Victor stands, power swelling.

For the first time, his SCAR SPLITS OPEN, revealing a METAL GLOW beneath the skin. He remains scary calm.

VICTOR
It's pronounced Latveria.
(looking down at the dead body)
This meeting's over, Ned.

Victor walks away, the final lights going to DARKNESS.

INT. VICTOR'S OFFICE - DAY

Victor enters, still adrenalized. He turns to the light switch, and the lights come on. He approaches his screens, and the monitors flicker to life. His powers are growing.

One MONITOR rolls the news. IMAGES of the FANTASTIC FOUR. Victor leans closer, and the VOLUME automatically goes up.

NEWSCASTER (ON TV)
...the Fantastic Four put on quite a show last night. They landed on every major headline in the northern hemisphere. In related news...

An IMAGE of VICTOR on screen.

NEWSCASTER (ON TV) (CONT'D)
Reports have surfaced that Von Doom Industries may be filing for bankruptcy. You may remember that it was Victor Von Doom who...

Victor turns away from the screen. The volume goes down. He focuses his eyes on REED.

Leonard enters, stepping closer, seeing the faint flicker of VICTOR'S METALLIC SCAR. His eyes narrow, concerned.

LEONARD
Sir, is everything okay? What happened to your..?

Victor keeps his eyes on the screens, totally engrossed.

VICTOR
(under breath, seething)
Reed... He got what he wanted...
(looking at Sue)
Everything he wanted...he took from me.

He leans ever closer, so the static starts to swallow Reed. A hard, deadly beat. Victor's eyes narrow, zooming into...REED'S RESEARCH: SLIDES on the wall. He zooms into key words:

DANGER, UNSTABLE IONS, MUTATION, OVERLOAD. And Victor gives a slow, thin smile. A new plan forming.

VICTOR (CONT'D)
Now I'm going to take it back. Piece by bloody piece...

His fist clenches. We hear METALLIC SFX.

INT. BAXTER BUILDING - TRANSFORMATION LAB - DAY

Reed enters the room carrying a stack of boxes that no normal man could balance. But he is not normal. His arms are wrapped around the boxes five times over— like human twine. He stops short, and drops the boxes when he sees...

VICTOR overseeing a troop of TECHNICIANS. They are boxing up Reed's work — all of his equipment, research. Victor wears a bandage, covering his scar. Reed eyes a glint of METAL.

REED
Victor, are you...are you okay?

Victor turns away.

VICTOR
Don't worry about me. Worry about yourself.

Reed looks around, seeing his lab turned inside out.

REED
What are you doing here?

VICTOR
What I should have done a long time ago.

VON DOOM INDUSTRIES

Production designer Bill Boes likes to describe the Von Doom Industries building as a gigantic tombstone: "My concept was something out of a giant graveyard, a slab with no decor, but a building that's also sleek and ergonomic. It all starts when Ben and Reed walk up to the building at the start of the film to ask Victor for financing for the space trip. The first thing you see is this thirty-foot high statue of Von Doom. We designed the statue in very dark colors, dark brown, with polished metal. The head alone is three feet high and we did a sculpture of Julian McMahon for it. I wanted the statue to tell us that Von Doom thinks the world is his domain — although it's funny because Ben and Reed joke about the statue being a sign of Von Doom's inadequacy."

According to Boes, things don't brighten up much inside. "The building is covered with glass, and the lobby is very dark and covered in polished concrete," he says. "I modeled the building after Trump Tower [the famous New York headquarters of tycoon Donald Trump] because it's surrounded by high finance, lots of money. I wanted to include all sides of New York, rich and poor, in the film. Even though Von Doom's building is dark and foreboding, it's also beautiful and opulent. I wanted the building to reflect Von Doom's self-importance, his wealth, that's he's a man who has everything and wants more."

A quick elevator ride up the fifty-story building, and the owner's secret office is revealed. It's a monument to Victor Von Doom. "I wanted the design to be full of Vs, so they're everywhere in the office. Plus, in the tradition of Jack Kirby, a lot of the shapes intersect," says Boes. "I also wanted it to be in the tradition of the lairs of the James Bond villains. It's opulent, but it's also full of straight lines, which reflect Von Doom's rigid personality. Victor and Reed are rivals from MIT, and their two domains — one messy, one clean and austere — reflect the contrast between the out-of-the-box-thinking of Reed and Victor's clear and simple approach."

Von Doom's office also offers some surprises for eagle-eyed fans, as well as hints of Von Doom's beloved home country, Latveria. "As an in-joke, there's a series of pictures hanging on the wall of Von Doom posing with various celebrities, including of course William Stryker from *X2*," says Boes. "The rest of the office, save for all the Vs, is pretty minimalist with the desk, chairs, table and console, but it all has a kind of gothic, Eastern European flavor as a clue to Von Doom's life in Latveria, our only clue really since Latveria doesn't actually feature in the movie. I also made a point of including the Latverian flag, with its red and green look, as a tribute to the Dr. Doom character because, you know, I actually kind of like Victor!"

Opposite: The tombstone-like Von Doom Industries building.

Above and left: Victor's office: a monument to one man's ego.

Applications and patents, Reed. This all belongs to me.

Reed reaches out, grabbing a folder from a box.

REED
But I'm not done with the machine—

VICTOR
Which is precisely the point. Analysis is over. It's time for action. My men could have mass-produced this by now.

Reed shakes his head, defending himself.

REED
Mass-produced? This isn't a toaster. You have no idea how it works.

Victor pulls the folder from Reed's hand, and whips out the intricate DIAGRAM of the MACHINE. He points to parts:

VICTOR
Re-create the storm, invert the polarity here, reverse the mutation there. Don't talk to me like I'm some schoolboy. I've got the same Phd you do.

Reed is a little surprised that Victor is so familiar with his machine. He points to a SECURE CHAMBER on the blueprint.

REED
The storm needs to be handled exactly right, or it could make our mutations worse, much worse, maybe even kill us...

Victor slows. Is Reed getting to him? Or giving him ideas?

REED (CONT'D)

Victor, please. We need time to verify the data... We can't afford any mistakes - there's only enough ions for two or three attempts.

Victor considers. He seems to enjoy watching Reed dangle.

VICTOR
Reed. I'm not asking permission.
(a final verdict)
We'll build it, while you check the specs.

Victor walks out. Reed looks unsure, as we CUT TO—

INT. BAXTER BUILDING TRANSFORMATION LAB - DAY

The SHIELDS slowly rise. FIVE TECHNICIANS go to work. They wear the VDI jackets. Reed watches, worried.

Sue enters. She sees the shields, the technicians, the VDI logo. And she is deeply worried. She steps over to Reed. Sparks fly behind them. Drills scream.

SUE
Can I talk to you?

INT. BAXTER BUILDING - REED'S OFFICE - DAY

Sue steps into the office, followed by Reed. Quiet, urgent:

SUE
Don't let Victor push you into making a mistake—

REED
He was going to take away all my data,

equipment—

SUE
Better than your life. Victor's not the one who has to get into that thing. We are.

Reed starts to snap, losing his studied cool.

REED
Which is why I'm working twenty hours a day, checking every variable—

SUE
Every variable but yourself. You don't eat, sleep. You can't live in your head like—

REED
(finally losing it)
I'm not the only one in there. I got you, Vic, Ben, Johnny, all rattling around in there.

Sue stands there, shocked by his outburst. A beat.

SUE
So clear it out. Get out of your head. Get out of here...

He looks at her, knowing what she means. Where she means.

EXT. BROOKLYN STREETS - DAY

Ben nearly knocks people over as he stomps down the street, mind tossing and turning. People stare, point. A LITTLE GIRL and FRIEND run up to him.

LITTLE GIRL
Mister, Mister! Please help me! My kitty is stuck in a tree.

She gestures to a tree next to Ben. Looks up.

LITTLE GIRL (CONT'D)
Please save Miss Lucy.

Ben rolls his eyes. Looks up. Considers climbing the tree, but thinks better of it. He has another idea...

Ben grabs the tree with one hand, and starts shaking the crap out of it.
MEEEEEEOOOOOOOOWWWWWRRRRRR!!!!

The cat falls into frame. At the last instant, Ben sticks out his hand and the cat lands safely in his palm. He hands the cat to the girl. Barely acknowledges her profuse thanks. He just moves on.

EXT. ANOTHER BROOKLYN STREETS - NIGHT

Ben passes a window in a gallery, and almost misses A LARGE SCULPTURE of his bust.

He stops, backs up to take a look. It's exquisitely rendered, capturing not just brute physicality, but the haunting anguish in his eyes. Ben is amazed, and touched, but...

BEN
(under breath)

Eyebrows are a little big...

A beat. He stares at these images of himself.

VOICE (O.S.)
I figured the only way to get you here was to stick that in the window.

He turns to see...ALICIA in the doorway.

BEN
How'd you know it was me?

ALICIA
I'm blind, not deaf. Wanna come in?

He steps toward her. But he sees...a PARTY in the back part of the gallery. Ben pauses, a little insecure.

BEN
I'm not really dressed for a party.

ALICIA
Relax, it's casual.

BEN
No, I mean...I'm a little...dusty...

She smiles, a thought forming, as we CUT TO—

INT. GALLERY - STUDIO - NIGHT

WHOOSH! A SCULPTOR'S HOSE sprays a thin stream of water at BEN. Alicia cleans Ben with her hands, using thin CARVING CHISELS for his cracks. Intricate, intimate work.

Ben enjoys every moment. He eyes a couple, large PUPPETS in the corner.

BEN
Those yours too?

ALICIA
My step-dad's. I'm strictly into stone. I was wondering when you'd walk by.

THE THING
You know, you could'a run an ad in the personals.

ALICIA
"Sensual blind chick seeks three-ton, rock-hard he-man for deep spiritual relationship."

THE THING
This ain't permanent. My friend Reed's working on a cure...I think.

She gets closer, running her hands across his arm.

ALICIA
Bennie. You feel pretty good <u>as is</u>.

Ben bristles. He doesn't want to stay this way.

THE THING
You don't know what it's like out there. Walking around like some kind of circus freak. People staring, whispering—

ALICIA
I wouldn't know anything about that.

THE THING
I mean...

ALICIA
Tell me. When you grew up in Brooklyn, how many astronauts did you know?
(a beat)
You went your own way then. You didn't listen to people. So why start now..?

As he ponders that, we a CROWD SWELLING on the CUT TO—

EXT. STREET - NIGHT

Fans swarm JOHNNY. He signs autographs, poses for pictures. Then his eyes move to...an incredibly long stretch LIMO. A tinted window rolls down. Victor's face emerges.

VICTOR
Need a ride, Johnny?

EXT/INT. LIMO - NIGHT

Johnny climbs in, sees...three impossibly gorgeous MODELS.

VICTOR
A few fans. Hope you don't mind.

JOHNNY
Gotta take care of the fans, right?

He smiles, sitting down in the middle of them.

VICTOR
Look, I built my business knowing what people

want. And right now, the people want you.

Johnny eyes the models, all lusting.

JOHNNY
And we don't want to let the people down now, do we?

VICTOR
No we don't. Which is why we need to strike while the iron's hot. I'm talking action figures, videogames, sponsors—

JOHNNY
Videogames? You serious?

Victor nods, knowing he has Johnny on the hook.

JOHNNY (CONT'D)
You talk to Reed and Sue about this?

VICTOR
Johnny. Let's be honest here. Ben, Reed, Sue. Good people, all. But stars?
(shaking his head, a beat)
I don't want to break up the band, but you're the one they want. Don't you think it's time to go solo..?

Victor subtly nods to the models. They envelop Johnny.

VICTOR (CONT'D)
Take the car for a spin. Think about it. Is this the life you want? Or would you rather live in Reed's lab..?

The car stops. Victor gets out. He stands on the pavement. As he shuts the door, we see the women climbing onto Johnny. The door shuts, and...

WHHHMMMPF! The windows all SUDDENLY STEAM UP!

EXT. HAYDEN PLANETARIUM - NIGHT

INT. HAYDEN PLANETARIUM - NIGHT

STARS on the ceiling. A VOICE drones about the galaxy. In the LAST ROW, we find: Reed and Sue. Reed is thinking about work.

REED
I could get Ben to tap into the Baxter's main power to generate enough voltage—

SUE
Reed. Shh. Just be quiet. And look up.

He slowly looks up. The stars seem to calm him.

SUE (CONT'D)
Remember our first date here..? God, I was so nervous.

REED
You were?

SUE
Of course I was. I'd read all your papers on bioethics. Some of them two times just so I'd have something to say to you.

Reed smiles softly, thinking back.

REED
You know, I bribed the projectionist ten bucks to keep it open late?

SUE
I gave him twenty.

They laugh. Sue looks up at the stars. Quiet:

SUE (CONT'D)
I didn't want that night to end.

Reed looks at her. Wrestles with a decision. Then quietly:

REED
Sue, you were right. It wasn't complicated. I just wasn't ready to be...to become...
(a beat)
You can be a little intimidating.

She knows. He trails off. Sue looks at him.

REED (CONT'D)
You always talked about how you liked the kind of man who could approach you...speak his mind. One who wasn't afraid to tell you what he wanted.

SUE
I did. I did, Reed... but I wanted you to be that man.

Someone SHUSHES them. They slump down further. Closer.

SUE (CONT'D)
When I walked out, I waited <u>ten minutes</u> out-side your door. Ten. Waiting for you to come find me.

REED
Why didn't you say something?

SUE
That would have kinda defeated the purpose. And Reed...
(closer, emotional)
I'm saying it now.

Their eyes lock. A heated beat. No more secrets. Their faces are close. A kiss is coming. Closer, closer. Sue disappears.

SUE (CONT'D)
(quiet, playful)
Come find me.

Reed tentatively leans into the kiss, and...

SUE (O.S.) (CONT'D)
That's my nose, genius... <u>These</u> are my lips.

Reed's face is SQUEEZED on both sides by Sue's invisible hands. She pulls him into a <u>KISS</u>. Lips touch. Soft, tender. Stars twinkle. And we slowly DISSOLVE TO—

EXT. KIRBY GALLERY - NIGHT

Ben and Alicia step out together. The crowd quiets, turns. A few whispers flutter. Alicia leans close to Ben, and slips her arm into his. The party goes back to normal.

ALICIA
Look around. I'll get us drinks. They always let blind girls cut the line.

She walks off. He watches her go. The way her hair moves. The lines of her neck. The light on her skin. This woman is the most beautiful thing Ben has ever seen. He's falling hard.

Ben steps through the crowd. The swanky guests give strained smiles, polite. Ben is start-ing to feel comfortable here. He keeps his eyes on Alicia, who talks to guests.

Ben hangs back, happy to watch her. A few patrons pass him, thinking he's just an inani-mate statue.

PATRON
I don't know about this one. It lacks a cer-tain...realism.

Ben keeps his eyes on Alicia. He overhears two BOHEMIAN GIRLS, who assume he's a statue.

BOHEMIAN GIRL#1
She's always had a thing for runaways and strays, but this is ridiculous.

BOHEMIAN GIRL #2
I know. Did she really think these sculptures would <u>sell</u>?

BOHEMIAN GIRL #1
Like anybody would want this <u>thing</u> in their

house. That girl's a one-woman charity.

Ben just stands there, frozen. His eyes dart around the room, paranoid now. Aware of peo-ple staring, laughing. He glances at Alicia, who giggles at something else. Ten seconds ago, this would have been dreamy. Now it's damning.

We stay with Alicia, who cuts through the crowd, emerging where she left Ben. She has a PITCHER of wine in hand for him. But Ben is <u>gone</u>. She looks disappointed, hearing his heavy FOOTSTEPS get softer and softer in the dis-tance.

THUNDER booms on the CUT TO—

EXT/INT. DINER - NIGHT

A pitstop in Queens. Heavy RAIN swims down windows. BEN sits at the COUNTER, with his hat pulled low, coat tight. Nobody sits within four chairs of him. He sips coffee in a metal bowl. A long beat. Then...

VICTOR (O.S.)
This seat taken?

Ben turns to see...VICTOR.

BEN
What are <u>you</u> doing here?

VICTOR
I'm worried about you.

BEN
About me? How sweet.

VICTOR
Come on. Let me buy you something to eat. Looks like you could use the company.

Ben considers. A man deeply alone. A beat.

INT. DINER - LATER

Victor and Ben sit in a window booth. A wait-ress sets a foothigh stack of pancakes in front of Ben, removes huge plates he's just cleaned. Victor's aware of the other customers in the diner staring at Ben. Ben burps: it rattles the plates.

THE THING
'Scuse me.

VICTOR
I know it can't be easy. Life hasn't changed that much for Reed, Sue and Johnny. At least they can go out in public. But for you? People star-ing. Whispering behind your back...

THE THING
If you're trying to cheer me up you're doing a helluva job—

VICTOR
I'm just saying, I know what it's like to lose something you love. To see it slip away, and know it's never coming back.

The Thing shoves a huge piece of pie in his mouth.

THE THING
Reed's gonna fix me up—

VICTOR
For your sake I hope you're right. I'm sorry if that sounds a little skeptical.

THE THING
Skeptical..?

Ben doesn't trust him. But Victor is hitting pressure-points.

VICTOR
Look, he's a brilliant man, we should trust he's working as hard as he can. You're his best friend. So what possible reason could he have for taking his time?
(a beat)
I mean, other than getting closer to Sue?

Off The Thing: a seed of doubt has been plant-ed. He can't help but hear some truth in the words. And we CUT TO—

Michael Chiklis
"For me, it's a huge turning point when Von Doom decides to put this maniacal bug in my ear about Reed and Sue not wanting to help me. It looks like Ben is going to be okay in his new skin when he meets this lovely girl, Alicia, who sort of becomes his girlfriend. But right on the heels of being mocked by some of her friends, he realizes it won't work, and becomes despondent again. He is then further taunted by Doom about the whole situation, and that throws him over the edge. He buys into it and that's why Doom is such an ugly villain, because he uses weakness to destroy friendships. He tries to create rifts within his 'family'."

INT. BAXTER BUILDING - TRANSFORMA-TION LAB - NIGHT

Reed and Sue return, laughing quietly, bodies close. Reed turns on the lights, and they flinch when they see...<u>BEN</u>. He sits waiting, scowling. They stop laughing immediately.

BEN
Yeah, I have that effect on people.

The construction of the TRANSFORMATION CHAMBER is complete. The Technicians are gone now.

REED
Ben—

BEN
Oh, you remember my name do you? You hap-pen to remember what you <u>swore</u> to do with every breath in your body?

REED
We're working as hard as we can—

BEN
Yeah. I can tell. Victor was right.

He motions to Reed and Sue together.

REED
Come on, this is nothing.

Sue looks a little hurt.

BEN
Glad "nothing" could take you away from your work.

REED
Ben, I don't know if this thing'll change us back or make us worse. I need you to be patient for a little while longe—

He POKES his finger into Reed's chest, which INDENTS around it like the Pillsbury Doughboy. Ben pushes Reed back. Hard.

BEN
Look at me, Reed. Look at me!

He grabs Reed's face, his fingers INDENTING the skin. He THROWS Reed back. Reed slams down to the ground.

REED
I am looking. That's why I can't make a mistake! I've got to get it right, and it's not right yet! We need to test this.

Ben shakes his head, looking down at Reed.

BEN
I spent my whole life protecting you, from the schoolyard to the stars. For what? So you could play Twister with your girlfriend while I'm the freak of the week?

Reed tries to stand, but Ben KNOCKS him back. Reed slams into the wall, and stays down this time.

SUE
Ben! Stop it! Or I'll stop it.

She starts to raise her hands to throw force-fields.

BEN
Stay out of this Susie.

As Ben turns to her, Reed takes this opportunity to WRAP Ben up like a python. They struggle. Ben runs back into a wall to shake Reed. Their faces are close, heated.

BEN (CONT'D)
Good thing you're flexible enough to watch your own back. 'Cause you're on your own now.

Ben seems to relax and Reed lets go. Ben walks out. Sue comes to Reed's side. He's bleeding.

REED
I'm OK. Just go, go after him. Stop him.

She heads out. Reed slowly stands. He looks at the transformation machine. It's not ready. But...Reed steps toward it. As he walks, his image goes grainy in—

INT. VICTOR'S OFFICE - NIGHT

Victor gets closer to his screens, watching Reed's every step. *This is what Victor has been waiting for*. His screens flicker with static — he's too close, but he can't pull back. He sees: REED TURNS ON THE MACHINE. Hits a countdown. And he grabs his UNIFORM...

INT. BAXTER BUILDING - HALLWAY - NIGHT

Sue hustles down the long hall. Ben turns a corner, passing the elevators, heading toward the FREIGHT ELEVATOR. She gets there too late. Doors close, going down.

INT. BAXTER BUILDING - GROUND FLOOR - NIGHT

Ben pounds across the lobby. He sees Johnny coming in.

JOHNNY
Christmas come early! Check it out!

He holds up an ACTION FIGURE of BEN: a horribly bloated body topped by a tiny pinhead. Johnny pushes a button and—

BEN ACTION FIGURE
IT'S CLOBBERIN' TIME!

WITH ONE ARM, Ben shoves Johnny into a wall. With his other hand, Ben grabs the toy and SMASHES it into the wall, inches from Johnny's head. The toy lodges into the plaster.

JOHNNY
Hey! That's a prototype!

BEN
Go back to the drawing board.

He strides away.

INT. BAXTER BUILDING - GROUND FLOOR - NIGHT

DING. Sue speeds out of the elevator. No sign of Ben. She runs into...JOHNNY who shakes off the encounter.

SUE
Johnny? Did you see Ben?

JOHNNY
Yeah, for the last time, I hope. I'm done with this freak show. I'm moving back to the real world.

SUE
Is that what you call it? "Real"?

JOHNNY
At least it beats living in a lab like somebody's science project.

This hits home. Sue is quiet. Johnny turns to go.

SUE
Johnny, slow down. Think. You know mom didn't raise us to—

JOHNNY
Look around, sis! She's not here. So you can stop talking to me like I'm your little boy—

SUE
As soon as you stop acting like one. Come on, you're smarter than this. You think those people out there care about you? You're just a fad to them.

He pulls away from her, taking a step out the door.

JOHNNY
Let's try something new: you live your life. And I'll live mine.
(beat)
And just for the record: they LOVE me.

He strides into the night, leaving Sue alone. A dark night. The Fantastic Four is no more. The family is split apart.

INT. BAXTER BUILDING - TRANSFORMATION LAB - NIGHT

The transformation chamber is up and running. Numbers count down. The storm swirls in the chamber. Reed now wears the UNIFORM. He opens the door:

HE'S GOING TO USE IT ON HIMSELF. HE IS FINALLY TAKING ACTION.

INT. VICTOR'S OFFICE - NIGHT

Victor sits enthralled. He leans forward, breathless.

INT. BAXTER BUILDING - TRANSFORMA-TION LAB - NIGHT

Reed gets closer. His heart races. So does Victor's. A moment of truth for both of them. REED STEPS INTO THE MACHINE.

Reed looks up at the cosmic storm. He opens his arms, ready to risk his life. And...WHHHM! He JOLTS in JUMP-CUT-MOTION, RECON-FIGURING, JERKING out of control, and we CUT TO—

VICTOR'S OFFICE - NIGHT

His screens GO BLACK. He looks out the window to see...a flash atop the BAXTER BUILD-ING! The tip of the Baxter glows. The rest of its lights GO OUT, FLICKERING in a power surge.

INT. BAXTER BUILDING - GROUND FLOOR - NIGHT

Lights go haywire. Sue knows immediately...

SUE
Oh god, Reed.

INT. BAXTER BUILDING -

TRANSFORMATION LAB - NIGHT

Lights flicker in darkness. The door rips open. Sue lunges inside. She sees through smoke and sparks...REED sways in the chamber. A beat. Did it work? Then...

Reed SLUMPS TO THE GROUND. His eyes flutter back. Dead..? His body is warped, twisted — one half remains tense, hard, while the other half is loose, soft, almost *melted* .

SUE
What did you do, Reed? What did you do?

INT. VICTOR'S OFFICE - NIGHT

Victor watches every second on his monitors.

**INT. BAXTER BUILDING -
TRANSFORMATION LAB - NIGHT**

Sue struggles to lift Reed — half of his body is STRETCHED OUT, devoid of any semblance of bone structure. One side of his face looks like it's MELTING OFF.

REED
I can...make it work.

SUE
Reed, stop, you need to rest your—

REED
The power...I need...more power...to control...the storm—

SUE
You <u>need</u> a doctor.

Reed loses consciousness. Sue carries him out.

INT. VICTOR'S OFFICE - NIGHT

Victor watches, his eyes narrow, looking at his hands.

VICTOR
More power..?

He reaches out for his phone, and...his SPEAKERPHONE <u>AUTOMATICALLY</u> TURNS ON. His powers growing.

VICTOR (TO PHONE) (CONT'D)
Leonard. <u>Bring me our lab rat.</u>

EXT. UNDER THE BROOKLYN BRIDGE - NIGHT

Ben sits alone, looking at city lights. A man without a home. Without a family. A hard beat. HEADLIGHTS slash across Ben. He slowly turns, blinded in the lights of...a LIMO.

LEONARD
Ben! They need you back at the Baxter building. It's...Reed.

Ben considers. Despite it all, he's a good friend. And a good man. As he gets into the car, we hear THROBBING MUSIC IN—

INT. MANHATTAN NIGHT CLUB - NIGHT

LOUD MUSIC and PULSATING LIGHTS. A young crowd dances and grinds to the beat. Among the colorful lights, STREAKS OF FLAME swirl around the ceiling. We follow them to:

A BALCONY, where we see JOHNNY sitting in a cozy VIP section. He's surrounded by "groupies" climbing over each other to get a look at his various parlour tricks.

He leans closer to a YOUNG WOMAN. Closer. CANDLES around them start to melt. Beads of sweat drip down her face.

JOHNNY
What do you say we get out of here?

She pauses. And...a very LARGE MAN steps up.

JOHNNY (CONT'D)
This your boyfriend?

The Boyfriend doesn't look too happy.

BOYFRIEND
Is that all you do? Bar tricks and stealing chicks...

Johnny does one more trick...taps the guy's drink...igniting it into a burst of flame. The Boyfriend drops the glass, which SMASHES on the ground...catches the floor on fire.

The boyfriend quickly moves in and stamps it out.

GIRLFRIEND
What are you doing?! You could have <u>burned</u> somebody!

The boyfriend takes his girlfriend's hand, they start to walk off. She turns back for one last comment...

GIRLFRIEND (CONT'D)
You know, if I had your power I'd be doing something with it, not wasting my time doing cheap bar tricks, hitting on some other's guy's girl.

Johnny looks a little embarrassed. The couple leaves. Johnny glances around. His FANS look down, away. He sees how quickly they can turn. The crowd parts slightly. He looks very alone.

INT. TRANSFORMATION CHAMBER - NIGHT

Leonard leads The Thing inside. The ominous chamber sits with its door open. Victor enters from the control station.

VICTOR
Ben, come in.

BEN
What is this? Where's Reed?

VICTOR
Where do you <u>think</u>? With <u>Sue</u>.

Ben looks at the flickering lights. Suspicious. Victor turns to Leonard, who looks a little scared by this dark room.

VICTOR (CONT'D)
(quiet)
I'll take it from here, Leonard.

Leonard nods, all too eager to get the hell out of here.

LEONARD
Yes sir.

Leonard disappears fast, as Victor turns back to Ben.

BEN
What do you want, Vic?

VICTOR
To help you. I've run every test known to man. And they all yield the same result: <u>the machine is ready</u>.

Ben shakes his head, wanting to believe, but...

BEN
Reed said it'd be weeks till—

VICTOR
He <u>also</u> said we'd avoid that storm in space. And we know how that turned out.

Ben nods. Reed <u>was</u> wrong before. Ben gets closer to the machine, drawn to it. He wants to believe, so badly.

VICTOR (CONT'D)
He couldn't generate enough power for the machine to reach critical mass. Yet another mistake for "Mr. Fantastic."

BEN
And you can? Power it up?

Victor stands in shadows, but we see the tiniest little SPARK around him. The lights..? Or his skin..?

VICTOR
Yes. I've found a new energy source.

He keeps his arm behind his back — his finger-tips course with ELECTRICITY. It starts to build, sparking up his arm.

VICTOR (CONT'D)
Tell me...<u>*do you want to be Ben Grimm again*</u>?

Ben keeps his eyes on the machine. His dream is alive.

BEN
Let's do it.

INT. TRANSFORMATION CHAMBER - NIGHT

The chamber doors open. Thing enters. He looks around this sterile box. An animal in a cage. Victor pushes a control; the doors of the chamber slowly close and seal. Thing shuts his eyes. He just wants to be Ben again.

FROM THE CONTROLS: Victor initiates the transformation sequence. As lights go on inside the chamber, they dim in the lab. Energy pumps into the chamber. The storm swirls faster. Lights flicker...there's not enough

power, until—

—Victor walks over...grabs hold of the machine with both hands...and WHHHM! A countdown begins in the control panels.

SLOW MOVE IN on the chamber, The Thing's face in the window. The chamber activates. The storm strikes hard.

The Thing opens his mouth, a beat, then he screams in agony. Struggling violently inside. To escape? Extend the moment: Condensation obscures the chamber window: The Thing vanishes.

EXT. MANHATTAN SKYLINE - NIGHT

The city lights fill the sky, and give it a quiet, eerie glow. Suddenly, a BRIGHT FLASH emerges from a window of the Baxter Building. The rest of the city lights dim slightly.

INT. BAXTER BUILDING LIVING QUARTERS - NIGHT

Reed lies in bed, weak, recuperating. When the power surges, we MOVE in on him: he looks up in alarm, knowing that someone's using the chamber. He starts to get out of bed, straining to stand with every muscle left in his body.

INT. BAXTER BUILDING - MEDICAL SUPPLY ROOM - SAME TIME

Sue sifts through a cabinet full of medications. The lights dim. Power failure. She looks up...

EXT. CLUB - NIGHT

Johnny walks alone. A WAVE OF LIGHT spreads through the sky. He looks up. His eyes adjust to the blast, as he realizes where it's coming from. He starts RUNNING toward the Baxter.

INT. BAXTER BUILDING - REVERSION LAB - NIGHT

INSIDE THE MACHINE, the RED CLOUD swirls with debris, crackling with light. The chamber rattles dangerously, as the power seems to SHAKE the very foundation of the building.

And then it's over. The light dies down...somewhat. It still pulses along with the chamber. The chamber door SLIDES OPEN.

Beat. And...BEN GRIMM steps out. Not The Thing. No more rocks. BEN GRIMM. Naked, tired, but finally A NORMAL MAN.

He slips on his trench-coat — now way too large. He collapses. He stares at his hands, his arms... it worked.

BEN
Oh my God...Th-thank you. THANK YOU... VIC?!

Ben sees a SPARK in shadows. That spark is...

VICTOR'S ARM. Victor steps forward, and

reveals himself to Ben: ELECTRICITY PUMPS THROUGH HIS BODY. His skin is part flesh, part metal. Cheekbone exposed, steel tissue.

HE IS DOOM.

BEN (CONT'D)
Vic... What the..?

DOOM
Everyone thought I was safe behind those shields...

BEN
Victor, the machine worked for me. It can work for you—

DOOM
It did, Ben. It worked perfectly.

Ben starts to realize...

BEN
You planned this..?

Doom smiles, reaches out his hand — ELECTRICITY builds from his shoulders, coursing down his arms to his fingertips.

DOOM
I've always wanted power. Now I've got an unlimited supply...

BEN
And no Thing to stand in your way.

DOOM smiles, nods, stronger than Ben now.

DOOM
Take a good look, Ben. This is what a man looks like who embraces his destiny.

Doom clenches his fist and BLASTS Ben, sending him flying backwards across the room — knocked unconscious.

DOOM (CONT'D)
One down, three to go.

Suddenly, WHOOSH! The lab door flies open. Reed enters. Doom steps back into the shadows.

DOOM (CONT'D)
Right on cue.

Reed's eyes go wide. He sees Ben crumpled in the corner.

REED
Oh god Ben. Are you okay?
(amazed)
You did it, you really did it...

DOOM
No, Reed. I did.

Reed slowly turns to see...DOOM. His body, his face.

REED
Victor..? What, what happened to you? What did you do to your—

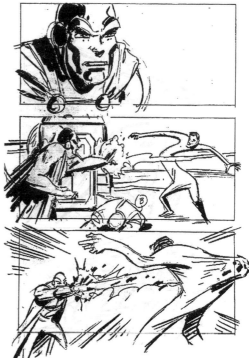

DOOM
<u>Exactly</u> what I <u>said</u> I would: I built a better,
stronger being. And outsmarted the great Reed
Richards—

REED
Victor, this isn't the way to—

DOOM
(a dark smile)
You always know best. So tell me. What happens when you superheat rubber?

Doom BLASTS an electrical BOLT at Reed,
KNOCKING Reed through the huge window!
Reed's body RUBBER-BANDS from the blast.

EXT. BAXTER BUILDING - NIGHT

Reed SLINKIES down the face of the building,
skin rippling.

**INT. BAXTER BUILDING - REVERSION
LAB - NIGHT**

Doom looks out the window, smiling at his old
friend's fall.

**INT. BAXTER BUILDING - FRONT LOBBY
- NIGHT**

DING! The elevator opens. Doom strides out.
He passes our friend O'HOOLIHAN, who looks
scared.

O'HOOLIHAN
Mr. Von Doom? Are you oka—

Doom casually SWIPES, sending him through
revolving doors.

DOOM
Never better, Jimmy. And it's <u>Doctor</u> Doom
now.

EXT. BAXTER BUILDING - NIGHT

Reed MELTS down the sides of an AWNING,
like a Salvador Dali watch. He tries to GRAB
HOLD of window ledges, but he can't get a
grip. His ARM streeetches, and SNAP! He falls
like a SLINKY, out of control. Half his body
loose, half hard.

He drips to the sidewalk, where...Doom steps
out. He catches Reed's face, holds it close.

DOOM
Why the long face?

Doom whips Reed into the night. As Doom
turns, people cower, horrified by his face. They
clear out, and...

Doom sees his REFLECTION in a window:
scarred skin, metallic veins. A monster.
Infuriated, he SHATTERS the window with an
iron fist, and bounds into the night.

INT. BAXTER BUILDING - LATER - NIGHT

Smoke billows, windows are shattered. Sue
races inside, seeing Doom's devastation.
Silence, deadly silence. Then...she sees a pile of
WRECKAGE shift. <u>BEN</u> crawls out.

SUE
Ben?!

She helps him out of the rubble. He is beaten,
battered.

JOHNNY (O.S.)
Sue!

Johnny comes running in. He sees the wreckage.

JOHNNY (CONT'D)
I'm sorry, sis, for leaving you guys—

SUE
No, <u>I'm</u> sorry, for pushing you out.

He nods. A beat between them. He looks
around, sees Ben.

JOHNNY
Jesus, Ben!
(eyeing him)
I go away, look what happens. You got a <u>lot</u> of
explaining to do.

He motions to the wreckage.

BEN
(struggling, weak)
The machine works. And Vic's gone Mister
Hyde on us—

JOHNNY
Really? With a name like Von <u>Doom</u>? Never
saw <u>that</u> one coming.

Sue looks around. Only one question. Dead serious:

SUE
Where is Reed?

BEN
Victor must've taken him.

INT. VON DOOM - CONFERENCE ROOM - NIGHT

Doom sits at the head of the table in an eerie parallel to the opening scene. Those mysterious CRATES loom in shadows. He wears a green HOOD, and METAL MASK over his scarred face.

Doom's eyes turn toward...the other end of the table.

DOOM
Chemistry 101, Part Two. What happens to rubber when it's super-cooled?

We now see what he sees: Reed sits in a chair with TUBES INJECTED into his skin FREEZING HIM SOLID! Ultra-cold vapor coats him. Doom steps closer, a sadistic smile.

Reed tries to move but can't even ball his hand into a fist.

DOOM (CONT'D)
Allow me.

He PRESSES DOWN on one of Reed's fingers, which makes a horrific CRACKING SOUND. Reed's face twists with pain.

DOOM (CONT'D)
Painful..?

Doom seems to enjoy every CRACK. He leans closer.

DOOM (CONT'D)
You don't know the meaning of the word.

Doom lets up on Reed and reaches into a crate, and pulls outs a military-issue ROCKET-LAUNCHER. He aims at the city skyline, locking onto his target: JOHNNY STORM.

DOOM (CONT'D)
But you will.

Johnny's HEAT SIGNATURE glows. The screen flashes: TARGET ACQUIRED. Doom looks back at Reed, his launcher aimed casually over his shoulder.

VICTOR
Flame off.

BOOOOM! He fires without looking! A MISSILE blasts into the sky. THE MISSILE LIGHTS UP THE DARK NIGHT beginning its wide turn towards its target.

INT. BAXTER BUILDING

Johnny, Ben, and Sue hear the missile being fired and turn to the window - it BANKS,

coming STRAIGHT for them. They move to—

EXT. BAXTER BUILDING BALCONY - NIGHT

Johnny rushes toward the edge, to get a good look at the missile streaking closer. As he moves, the missile SHIFTS slightly with HIS MOTION! His eyes narrow, thinking.

He FLAMES ON a HAND. He waves his flaming hand, and the MISSILE locks onto the fire! Johnny darkens, realizing...

JOHNNY
Great. Heat-seeker.

His mind races. He makes a decision, and steps up onto the ledge, hundreds of feet above the street.

SUE
What are you doing—

JOHNNY
Sis. Let me take care of you for once.

SUE
But Johnny...you can't fly.

Johnny considers, a half-beat. He looks out. Under breath:

JOHNNY
Well then this'll be one hell of a basejump.

Sue reaches out to stop him, but Johnny DIVES HEROICALLY OFF THE EDGE! He FLAMES ON! The missile follows his arc. As he drops, his clothes BURN OFF, revealing his UNIFORM.

JOHNNY (CONT'D)
(under breath)
Come on...come on...come on....

He falls lower, lower. And...he...BANKS! SWOOPS UP! FLYING!

JOHNNY (CONT'D)
FLAME ON.

Sue watches, with fear, and a hint of pride.

BEN
We need to help Reed—

Sue shakes her head, sympathetic.

SUE
Ben, you got what we all wanted. You need to stay here. It's too dangerous.

She heads off. Ben watches her go, helpless.

INT. BAXTER BUILDING - REVERSION LAB - NIGHT

Ben steps back into this ravaged room. Through the shattered window, he sees Johnny's FLAMES streaking away. A hard beat.

BEN
What...what have I done?

EXT. NEW YORK - NIGHT

Johnny zigs and zags, but the missile takes every twist and turn, gaining on him, bearing down. Cars slow, stop. More people look up, scared, pointing at this stunning sight.

INT. VON DOOM CONFERENCE ROOM - NIGHT

Eerily silent. Reed tries to move, but he is FROZEN. He hears a footstep. But the room is EMPTY. No sign of Doom even. A beat. He hears a CREAK. Another CREAK, closer. And...

A FREEZING TUBE starts to SHIFT. It goes taut, clearly being manipulated by a hand — an INVISIBLE HAND. Sue APPEARS next to Reed, tube in hand. She tries to stay calm.

SUE
What has he done to you?

Reed's eyes shift to see...Doom emerge from the darkness.

DOOM (O.S.)
How romantic.

SUE
Victor, please—

DOOM
It's Doctor Doom to you.

He steps closer. Electrodes course over his metal skin.

SUE
We know the machine works. It worked on Ben, it'll work on you. We can turn you back—

DOOM
Do you really think fate turned us into gods so we could refuse these gifts?

She hardens, a little force field starts to emanate from her.

SUE
Victor. You always thought you were god.

Doom has a hand behind his back, generating an energy blast.

DOOM
Sue please, let's not fight.

SUE
No, Victor... Let's.

She HURLS a force-field at him. It CONNECTS, KNOCKING him back a half-step. But he simply shakes it off, and steps up. Too powerful. He smiles. His arms CRACKLE with electricity.

DOOM
Susan......You're fired.

BOOM! He FIRES an ELECTRIC SHOCKWAVE that LAUNCHES her back. She spirals

through the air, crashing into the wall, THUD-
DING to the floor. As Doom stalks closer, Sue
gathers her strength to...GO INVISIBLE.

DOOM (CONT'D)
Marco...

A hanging beat. We see: a FAINT OUTLINE of
Sue behind him.

DOOM (CONT'D)
Polo.

He SPINS, GRABS her! Doom grips her neck,
SLAMMING her to the ground beside Reed.
She lays there, beaten, visible.

In the distance behind Doom, city lights
BLINK, fading in and out. Lights flutter softly
here (like when Ben went through the
machine). Reed looks up. Could it be..?

EXT. EAST RIVER - NIGHT

Johnny jets over the water with the missile only
twenty feet behind him. He's running out of
options, when he spots:

A GARBAGE BARGE floating in the water
ahead. Thinking fast, Johnny does a fly-by and
HURLS a fireball at the barge. VWOOSH! The
flames ignite and spread quickly.

He loops back toward the flaming barge as the
missile closes in on him. Fifteen feet...ten...
Just as it's about to hit—

JOHNNY FLAMES OFF and falls toward the
water. As he tumbles through the air, we CUT

BACK TO—

**INT. VON DOOM CONFERENCE ROOM -
NIGHT**

From their vantage point, they see the missile
explode. Flames dance. Sue's eyes darken, as
Doom grips her neck.

Reed tries desperately to move, but he is
FROZEN. It takes every last ounce of strength
to lift one finger, which makes a CRACCCK-
KKKING sound.

DOOM
One more down. Now it's just the scientist and
his specimen.

Sue and Reed lock eyes. Reed tries to move his
mouth. He has something to tell her, struggling
just to move his lips and get the words out.

REED
Sue. The only thing I ever knew without thinking was...
(his lips fully freezing)
I...love...

He starts to say "you," but his lips FREEZE,
mid-word. Sue whispers to him:

SUE
Me too, Reed.

Doom steps towards Sue, about to deliver the
final blow.

DOOM
(quiet, cruel)

And so four became none. It's my time now.

BOOOOM! An elevator DOOR FLIES INTO
THE ROOM! SMASH!

VOICE (O.S.)
Actually, Vic...

Reed recognizes the voice. So do we. Doom
turns to see...

BEN GRIMM, AKA THE THING. Back in
rocky, fighting form.

BEN
IT'S CLOBBERING TIME!

Doom turns, just as—

BAM! Ben HITS Doom harder than any living
thing has ever been hit. The force sends Doom
back through the air, toward the far wall, where
he SMASHES into the massive "V" sculpture.
It SNAPS, crashing onto him. A few sparks.
Then nothing .

Nothing at all. No more movement. Doom is
dead.

Ben turns to Reed.

BEN (CONT'D)
Damn, I've been wanting to do that.

Reed manages the thinnest smile as Ben starts
disconnecting the tubes from Reed.

BEN (CONT'D)
(Reed's words)

Victor's "not that bad," huh? Just "a little larger than life"? Maybe you'll listen to me next time before—

WHMM! The WRECKAGE shifts. They turn to see...Doom EMERGES. He stands, power coursing. And he CHARGES at Ben! Ben charges back. And these two behemoths...

SLAM INTO EACH OTHER, CRASHING THROUGH GLASS, INTO THIN AIR!!

EXT. VON DOOM BUILDING - CONTINUOUS

Doom and Ben PLUMMET, wrestling in mid-air. On the ground, PEOPLE scream and duck for cover. Doom and Ben SMASH through the large GLASS roof of a lower building across

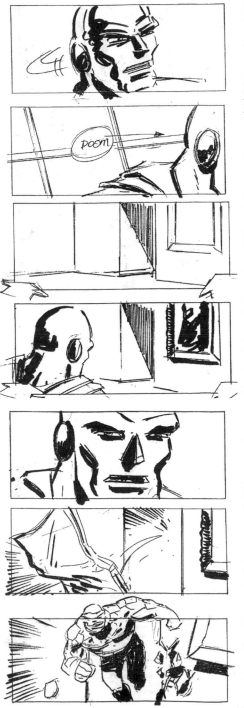

the street.

INT. HOTEL - INDOOR POOL - CONTINUOUS

BOOOOM! Doom and Ben, locked in combat, drop through the glass, landing in a large HOTEL POOL. People scream, run.

INT. HOTEL - INDOOR POOL - NIGHT

UNDERWATER: Doom and Ben LAND HARD. Their combined weight CRACKS the floor of the pool. A YOUNG BOY watches underwater through his MASK. Doom and Ben square off, but...

The CRACKS OPEN WIDER! And they're PULLED toward the HOLE! WHOOSH! The water is all sucked out of the hole. The boy holds tight to a ladder, as Ben and Doom crash down to—

INT. HOTEL - HALLWAY - NIGHT

A HOTEL GUEST sees water FLOOD into the hall. Roaring rapids head straight for him. He jams his key into the lock, turning desperately, just barely leaping out of the way as the wave carrying BEN and DOOM SMASHES through a window to—

EXT. HOTEL - CONTINUOUS

SMASH! Ben and Doom fly out the window, thrashing in the TEN-THOUSAND-GALLON WATERFALL TO—

EXT. NEW YORK CITY STREET - CONTINUOUS

CRASH! Water floods the street. Doom and Ben land in a large GARBAGE TRUCK. The truck rocks back and forth, DENTING from the inside. Grunts, growls.

CRASH! The truck suddenly STOPS. COP CARS SPEED CLOSER, sirens screaming. And—

BOOM, A HUGE SHAPE explodes from the truck. SMASH! Ben lands on a CAR filled with two OLD LADIES — his head cracks the WINDSHIELD. Doom steps out of the garbage truck, water flooding the street around him. COP CARS converge on Doom.

Doom turns his attention to the cops. His limbs SPARK with electricity, ready to fire at the cars.

EXT/INT. CAR - CONTINUOUS

Ben sees the cops and Doom. He knows the cops are dead meat. He turns to the OLD LADY in the driver's seat.

BEN
Excuse me, Maam. Can I borrow your car?

She nods and quickly gets out, shaking.

OLD LADY
The clutch sticks a little.

BEN
Not gonna be a problem.

Ben LIFTS the car and THROWS it at Doom. WHMM! It FLIES through the air, and WHAM! Hits hard, knocking Doom back twenty feet! As Doom FLIES back, a BUS enters frame, and—

EXT. NEW YORK CITY STREET - NIGHT

BOOM! Doom SMASHES into the OUT OF SERVICE BUS! CRASH! Windows shatter. The bus SLAMS into an ELECTRICITY POLE, snapping the pole. Doom steps out, unharmed.

Ben CHARGES toward him. Doom grabs the broken ELECTRICITY POLE, FLIPS it into his hand, and wields the pole like a giant STUN-GUN! Electric sparks FLY through the air into—

BEN! The BLAST of VOLTS launches him off his feet! He goes FLYING backward, ELECTROCUTED in mid-flight, and—

WHOOMPF! Ben LANDS HARD, face down, CRATERING the street! Water rushes into the crater. Ben lays there, incapacitated.

EXT. NEW YORK CITY STREET - SAME TIME

SOUND BITES

Julian McMahon
"The hardest part of filming for me was when I was wearing the heavy prosthetic suit and they put prosthetic scars all over my neck and face. I couldn't perspire at all, not one bit, so as not to destroy the effect, so I had to stand out in the freezing cold of Vancouver during winter for those scenes, just trying not to sweat. I was more worried about sweating than freezing to death."

On the street, cars SCREAM to stops, people GASP. Doom strides up to Ben, and raises the ELECTRICITY POLE for the death-blow. Currents surge. Right before he swings down—

VOICE (O.S.)
I can't let you do that.

Simple, strong. Doom turns to see...REED. Alone. Bruised and battered. Slowly stepping toward him. Doom smiles.

DOOM
And you can't stop me.

He turns back to Ben, raises the pole, but...he CAN'T SWING DOWN! Something is HOLDING the pole in mid-air.

Something *invisible*.

DOOM (CONT'D)
Hello Susan.

In the last act of the film, the Fantastic Four band together to combat the deranged Dr. Doom. In the streets of New York, the Four wage an epic battle inside and out of the Von Doom Building, summoning every bit of their powers to defeat their former colleague. In terms of size and scope, Tim Story says it closely rivaled the Brooklyn Bridge scene from the first act: "This was the sequence that actually shows all the guys in their uniforms, fighting and doing what they do, so it was the time to kind of go crazy with the effects. We wanted to show the complete package. This sequence needed to be the calling card for the movie, and the pinnacle of what we had been introducing all along. Sue is using all of her powers. Ben is going toe-to-toe with Doom. You have to show that Victor is now totally Dr. Doom, and giving everything he's got without apology. I knew this had to be at the highest level of effects work."

This spread: The showdown with Dr. Doom. "This scene needed to be the calling card for the movie," says director Tim Story.

Explaining the process and challenges of the final battle, Story says, "In shooting it, once again this was just like the bridge sequence in that it was completely difficult. We were outside in the elements again, where it rained, and it was at night. At the same time, I had major explosives, and a bus that was being thrown across a street. There is also a lot of water in the sequence, because Ben and Doom fall out of one building into a swimming pool in another. We had 350 extras, and more explosions with police cars and wire rigs. Once again, we threw everything at it to make it close to impossible, but the sequence really came out great."

The scene also finally brings the potential of the characters to fruition, with no-holds-barred action that hasn't been seen from the team, as a whole, until this climactic fight. "What you get is some kick-ass fighting from all four of them against Dr. Doom," Story continues. "I wanted to make sure we accomplished that, because when you look at the Fantastic Four in the comic books, they're not always fighting. Actually, it's very hard to create the perfect fight with these guys [all working together at once]. It's weird, because they aren't really set up for that dynamic. However, we were able to show an extremely active sequence. It has so much action in it! You see the four of them come together — because the story is really about the family breaking up, and then coming back together to face a common enemy. We were able to establish that and I have to say, I love what has happened with this sequence. It is so impressive to me, and seeing it with effects just gives you another ball of energy and a shot in the arm. So much of this movie is about doing things and hoping it looks right. You are kind of out there rolling the dice, but everybody went for it in this sequence. All four of them look great in their costumes, and Doom looks great in his. We really went for it and hopefully it will make the fans happy."

She turns VISIBLE, holding back the pole with a FORCEFIELD. Using her power, she FLINGS the pole from Doom's grip. It skids along the street. Reed helps Ben to his feet.

Doom turns to these three wounded soldiers.

DOOM (CONT'D)
What is this? The pitiful three?

Doom steps toward them, but—

VOICE (O.S.)
Four.

WHOOOSH! Johnny SWOOPS DOWN, hurling a FIREBALL like a flamethrower, KNOCKING Doom back.

Johnny takes his place alongside the others. *The four of them stand as one* . Johnny turns to Thing.

JOHNNY
Had a little relapse, huh?

Thing starts to retort, but Johnny gives a warm smile.

JOHNNY (CONT'D)
Welcome back.

They turn to Doom, who stands with metal skin slightly singed and melted, making him look all the more menacing.

DOOM
This is going to be fun.

Electricity starts to course through his body. He stands at the foot of the crater Ben made. He THRUSTS down, grabbing a thick POWER CABLE, RIPPING it out of the street!

He SNAPS the cable into two snaking, lashing strips. He holds tight, ABSORBING the power. Lights FLICKER and DIM in buildings around him. Windows BLOW! Doom GLOWS, amped up.

He LETS GO of the cables! The two deadly wires SNAKE out of control! PEDESTRIANS scatter, panic. Reed sees the wires SLASHING through the air. He makes a move:

Reed STREEETCHES HIS ARMS, reaching for the deadly cables.

Doom FIRES superpowered ENERGY BOLTS. The electric charges surge through the air toward the Fantastic Four, but—

Sue TOSSES her FORCE-FIELDS, exploding Doom's blasts in mid- flight. She keeps her hands up, BLOCKING blows like a prize- fighter. One of Doom's BOLTS glances off her force-field and—

SMASHES into a concrete stanchion of a BUILDING! The pillar starts to crumble, with PEOPLE huddled under the overhang! They're about to be CRUSHED by the falling concrete! But—

Suddenly, the concrete roof HOLDS STEADY...because...BEN is holding it up! He stands beside the stanchion, like Atlas holding the world. People run out, safe.

ON THE STREET: Reed finally grabs both ends of the wire.

REED
JOHNNY! SPOT-WELD!

Johnny FLIES toward him, and uses his flames to WELD the wires back together. Sparks fly. The cables start to FUSE.

Doom keeps FIRING. Sue struggles with her force-fields. The impact is too much. Her nose starts to bleed.

SUE
Can't...hold...on...

Doom smiles. Reed sees her. She is about to drop her hands, vulnerable, but..............REED STRETCHES HIS WHOLE BODY!

He EXPANDS himself across the street, and GRABS a TREE, so he forms a WALL between Sue and Doom.

Doom keeps FIRING his bolts. They SLAM into Reed's body, RUBBERBAND his skin, and DISTEND OUT his back without breaking. He strains, agonizing.

REED
Johnny. SUPERNOVA.

JOHNNY
But all these people...

REED
Now.

Johnny charges toward Doom — flames on his body starting build to a blinding white intensity, ENGULFING everything. Johnny GRABS DOOM.

THING
(quiet, smiling)
Flame on, kid.

FLASH! Johnny explodes in a PULSE of BRIGHT WHITE LIGHT, which starts to HEAT UP everything surrounding it. Reed doesn't miss a beat. He's in total command now.

REED
Sue, I need some of that anger, rage, frustration—

SUE
(looking at Doom)
I'm sure I can come up with something.

She concentrates. She sees Johnny holding onto Doom — and the GROWING HEAT and LIGHT.

Sue shuts her eyes. A GIANT FORCE FIELD EXPLODES FROM HER BODY. A massive WAVE OF ENERGY. It SWOOPS past a car, which WARPS, MELTS (half the car is not inside the force-field).

Thing turns to the crowd, extending his arms, blocking them.

Sue's force-field ENVELOPS JOHNNY'S SUPERNOVA, containing it in a BRIGHT SPHERE OF ENERGY. The light increases, to the point that it's blinding. People look away.

Finally, Johnny's supernova fades. He collapses to the ground, exhausted, smoking. Sue exhales and falls to her knees. Her force field fades. The light flickers out. As everyone's eyes adjust, we hear...THUD. THUD. And—

DOOM steps through the smoke. Unharmed. His metallic body GLOWS WHITE, TRAILING MOLTEN METAL. Sue, Ben, Johnny look devastated. They can't beat him. He looks at Reed.

DOOM
Is that the best you can do..? A little heat..?

Reed stays perfectly calm. He shakes his head.

REED
Time for your lesson, Vic. Chem 101: what happens when you supercool hot metal..?
(to Ben)
Ben...

BEN
Got it, teach.

He KICKS OPEN the FIRE HYDRANT. The water GEYSERS UP! Ben kicks down with his foot, deflecting the water so it sprays toward Reed, who...TWISTS HIS TORSO so...

The water CURLS around his chest, RACES down his arms, and SHOOTS right off his wrists toward Doom!

DOOM
No.

Doom RUSHES TOWARD Reed, but the WATER FLIES OUT, DOUSING DOOM. GIANT CLOUDS OF STEAM fill the air from the cooling metal. DOOM screams. His shrieks finally fade to SILENCE.

The water stops, thick steam clouds roll, completely obscuring Doom from view. A beat. The steam clears to reveal:

DOOM. A true statue now — a hard, cold solid piece of METAL. Frozen forever. Reed, Sue, Ben, and Johnny — *The Fantastic Four* — exhale. They stand as one, in roiling smoke. A beat.

JOHNNY
Damn, I love this job.

Reed and Sue slowly lock eyes, thinking the same thing.

BEN
Job, huh..?

Will they accept their mantle? Reed shrugs.

REED
Well, we do have the suits...

They give weary smiles. A team. Sue gets close to Reed.

SUE
You know, about what we said up there, I think maybe—

THHM! He KISSES HER. His neck extending. Strong, powerful. He pulls back slightly, smiles at her. A new strength in him.

BEN
Funny how things turn out, isn't it?

Sue looks at Reed. A long way from that conference room.

SUE
Hilarious.

As they kiss, people emerge, stepping out of hiding. The sun rises around them. The Fantastic Four step into the dawn of a new day. And we slowly DISSOLVE TO—

INT. CIRCLE LINE BOAT - BANQUET ROOM - DUSK

Reed and Sue kiss on the deck of the Circle Line as it chugs around New York City.

JOHNNY (O.S.)
Dude, that's still my sister.

A PARTY IN PROGRESS. Drinks, food, music. We see in the crowd a few familiar faces: O'HOOLIHAN (cast on his arm), bartender ERNIE, others. JOHNNY and BEN stand

behind Reed and Sue.

Reed and Sue pull apart. Reed turns to Ben, excited.

REED
Ben, I've been crunching the numbers on the machine. I think if we can rework the power settings...

BEN
Forget it, egghead. I'm good as is.

ALICIA (O.S.)
That's my Benny.

She hands Ben a big METAL MUG. Ben takes the mug. He CLINKS, but SHATTERS her glass.

ALICIA (CONT'D)
We're going to have to work on your touch.

BEN
I like the sound of that.

Alicia gets close. A soft smile. Reed turns to Sue.

REED
Sue, can I talk to you for a second?

Reed leads her out. Ben and Johnny swap a glance.

EXT. CIRCLE LINE BOAT - DECK - DUSK

A romantic view of the city-scape. Reed stands with Sue.

REED
I found a broken gasket, from space—

SUE
A gasket? Reed, we're at a party.

He opens his hand, revealing a circular piece of metal, just about the size of......a RING. Sue slows down.

REED
If one of us were to wear it...

MAKING MUSIC

A movie soundtrack can define a character, help drive a scene, or set a mood, and nobody excels at it like John Ottman. As one of Hollywood's most prolific composers, he has provided scores for a diverse range of films such as *Bubble Boy*, *Halloween: H20*, *Cellular* and *Hide and Seek*. He is also known for his long association with director Bryan Singer, having worked on *Apt Pupil*, *The Usual Suspects* and *X2*. Now the music maestro is lending his considerable talents to *Fantastic Four*, a movie Ottman chased down himself.

"I heard about the project and it sounded really exciting, so I called Ralph Winter, who was the producer on *X2* and was doing *Fantastic Four*," recalls Ottman. "I told him how much I wanted to be involved because

Above: The storm attacks the space station, to the accompaniment of John Ottman's score.

it sounded like a blast. He was instrumental in getting me in contact with the director, Tim Story, who I had a meeting with. Prior to that, they had given me a script. It was just making a couple of phone calls and, from there on, it was about talking to the music executives over at Fox. My enthusiasm meant a lot to them."

After scoring *X2*, Ottman has some insight into why superhero adventures are so creatively rewarding. "What is fun about it is you can let your hair down and do a lot of expository music that doesn't have to try and hide behind sensitive dialogue," he explains.

"There are those moments of course, but nevertheless, there will be big sequences where you can let the orchestra rip. That is definitely one of the fun things."

Another plus seems to be that a *Fantastic Four*-sized budget allows a more impressive orchestra for the soundscape. "The greatest thing about that is basically you can have whatever orchestra you want to have," Ottman says. "You don't have to worry about trying to supplement the orchestra with some synthesized elements, which take a lot of time to design, to support the score. Sometimes, if they can't afford a certain large brass section, you might have to add some synthesized brass in there. It takes a long time to mix that in and manipulate it to sound right. But if you know you have a full orchestra at your disposal, you can actually write faster, because the initial demo version I create doesn't have to sound perfect — I know it's ultimately going to be performed by real musicians."

Fantastic Four obviously has multiple heroes, but that doesn't necessarily mean they all get the same musical attention. "You don't always have a theme for every single character, because sometimes that would be too convoluted," Ottman notes. "But in a comic book film, you probably will have at least mini themes or motifs for the main characters, and one scene that encompasses all of them. Same with *X2*. The X-Men theme reflects all of them, and some choice X-Men had miniature themes which reflected them. That will be the same for *Fantastic Four*."

Scoring is of course one of the last stages in the making of a film, and when he was interviewed for this book, Ottman hadn't yet seen the finished cut of the movie which acts as his main source of inspiration. Although he's read the script, apparently it doesn't paint the whole picture. "No, I wish it did though," he laughs. "I'd be a lot less stressed out right now! I haven't even started writing yet. There's a couple of scenes I can kinda hear the music in my head a little, but I'm hearing action elements, and I'm not sure what themes are going to be woven through that. There's the scene where a storm attacks the space station and I'm like, 'Oh God! That is gonna be so fun to score!' but that's about as far as I've gotten..."

She sees Johnny and Ben inside, watching — in on a secret.

Reed looks her square in the eye. Unflinching.

SUE
Reed. What are you doing?

Reed drops to his knees. His head stays eye-level, while his body drops. Sue gapes, so emotional she starts to DISAPPEAR.

REED
No more thinking, no more variables... Sue Storm...will you...
(she's gone)
Sue? Sue? You there?

Dead silence. And then...

THE RING DISAPPEARS. SUE IS WEARING IT.

SUE (V.O.)
Yes.

Reed goes to kiss her.

SUE (V.O.) (CONT'D)
That's my nose, genius... These are my lips.

Reed's face is SQUEEZED on both sides by Sue's invisible hands. She pulls him into a KISS and reappears.

INSIDE: the party applauds. Ben, Johnny and Alicia move through the crowd to join Reed and Sue. As they go—

BEN
No more cracks about how I look.

JOHNNY
Hey, I'm Mr. Sensitivity now.
(weaving around bodies)
Clear the way, wide load coming through.

Ben glares, fists clenched. Johnny smiles, mischievous, as they hit the balcony. And he FLAMES ON, taking off into the air, blazing the NUMBER "FOUR" enclosed in a circle of flame (their future callsign), over the city skyline. The crowd oohs and aahs. Ben watches, unimpressed.

BEN
Showoff.

People drink, laugh, dance. We slowly PULL BACK from the party, the boat, the city, and...CUT TO—

EXT. HARBOR - DAY

CLOSE ON: the MELTED FACE of DOOM. He is placed in a wooden crate. LEONARD oversees the operation, listening to his cell.

As two workers move the heavy door in place - a crackle of ELECTRICITY moves over Doom's body. Leonard's CELLPHONE goes STATICKY. His eyes narrow. Could it be..? And—

SLAM. The door closes. We can read the destination through stenciled lettering: LATVERIA. And we pull back to reveal the box is on the deck of:

A FREIGHTER SHIP. The ship pulls away, steaming into the horizon, as we...

FADE OUT.

THE END